REMI

Caitlin Press Inc.
3375 Ponderosa Way
Qualicum Beach, BC V9K 2J8
www.caitlinpress.com

Text design by Vici Johnstone
Cover and illustrations by Chrissy Courtney
Edited by Holly Vestad
Printed in Canada

Caitlin Press Inc. acknowledges financial support from the Government of
Canada and the Canada Council for the Arts, and the Province of British
Columbia through the British Columbia Arts Council and the Book Publish-
er's Tax Credit.

Title: Remnants : reveries of a mountain dweller / Natalie Virginia Lang.
Names: Lang, Natalie Virginia, author.
Identifiers: Canadiana 20220440743 | ISBN 9781773861043 (softcover)
Subjects: LCSH: Sumas Mountain (B.C.) | LCSH: Human ecology—British
Columbia—Sumas Mountain. |
    LCSH: Mountain life—British Columbia—Sumas Mountain. | LCGFT:
Creative nonfiction. | LCGFT:
    Essays.
Classification: LCC PS8623.A52285 R46 2023 | DDC C814/.6—dc23

REMNANTS

Reveries of a Mountain Dweller

by
Natalie Virginia Lang

CAITLIN PRESS 2023

For those who came before and those yet to arrive.

I respectfully acknowledge that I wrote this book on the unceded Traditional Territories of the Semá:th People of the Sumas First Nation, the Matsqui First Nation and the Stó:lō Nation. Stó:lō peoples have lived in this area for over ten thousand years; they are the original caretakers and custodians of this Land. I am grateful for their knowledge and wisdom through which I have come to learn so much.

CONTENTS

Fall 102

Winter   158

The mountain sat upon the plain

In his eternal chair,

His observation omnifold,

His inquest everywhere.

The seasons played around his knees,

Like children round a sire:

Grandfather of the days is he,

Of dawn the ancestor.

"The Mountain," Emily Dickinson (1896)

It's peaceful beneath the canopy; tranquil and unassuming. A deep belly breath brings the dewy morning air that follows a rainy night into my system; I am drunk on the freshness. It permeates my bloodstream, running up and down the meridians of my body, forcing sensory reflexes to awaken. I am attentive to a complete body and mind shift that only this place provides me. I feel taller yet less imposing. I feel wider yet nimble and light. I am utterly expansive as I tune into the rhythm of the forest. My skin tingles with goosebumps, tiny hairs stand up at the back of my neck, my head grows slightly fuzzy and my limbs move into a realm of weightlessness. I am carried along by some unseen army of forest elves beckoning me to experience spring on Sumas Mountain...

DEAR READER

What have I created for you in these pages? What words, what thoughts, what images will capture and hold you?

Sitting down to write in the space of stolen hours, I did not at first know what it was that I was writing. It began with an observation, in a very Rousseauian or Montaignian way: I captured shifting perspectives of a tree near my house. Then, I wrote about the swallows who chirp and glide in spring, and then it was a consideration of the rain and heat and the names we give. I thought at one time that I was writing what was known of my family history. At another time, it was of the heartbreak that comes with change. Finally, I found I was documenting the emotional state of a single year. A year that brought—alongside extraordinary joy and beauty—sensations of confusion, frustration, disillusionment and sadness.

I wrote and continued to write until it was time to stop. I wrote what I saw and what I felt. I wrote the experience of my life in the glisten of a singular place, in a singular time so saturated with progress and growth and greed and questions about sustainability and the protection of those places—with no acceptable answer.

What you will find here is a series of observations culminating mostly within the year 2021. The myriad of calamitous events throughout the Fraser Valley, BC, and around the world during that time have drawn great attention to the problem of climate change and our influence upon it. My response, my way of working to understand and talk about these issues, arose as a collection of questions and a commentary of hope for humanity—situated in present and historical place, dedicated to the intrinsic sparkle of ecology set against those inherent contradictions of what it means to be human. What it means to both contribute to a problem and work to solve it.

This contradiction is showcased through four seasons organized into four sections. I begin with spring—lightness, revitalization and change—and end with winter—the reflective quiet among the harsh realities of colder months, made even harsher by extreme weather. My aim is to showcase the wonder existing within these seasons as well as the broken-hearted realities of human growth and development.

It is with deepest gratitude that I thank you for picking up this book; I hope there is something here that may capture and hold you.

In the Beginning

In early 1900, the McLeod brothers, great-, great-uncles of mine on my mother's side, made their way from Scotland through Boston to Vancouver, and then up to the Nahanni Valley in the Dehcho Region of the Northwest Territories in search of gold. The valley became known as the Valley of the Headless Men and the McLeod brothers were the reason.

The Nahanni River flows for 563 kilometres, beginning at the Mackenzie Mountains, through the Selwyn Mountains and emptying into the Liard River, one of the largest watersheds globally, just north of the intersection of the Yukon, NWT and BC borders. The valley consists of gorges up to 900 metres deep, hot springs, four canyons over 420 metres high, lakes, the Virginia Falls—twice the height of Niagara Falls—and an otherwise inhospitable wilderness that has captivated Western audiences since the turn of the nineteenth century, when gold prospectors started travelling to the area. The Nahanni Valley is shrouded in supernatural lore: this is a place where curses may be real and where legends of murder, mystery and ghosts are born.

The Nahanni Butte Dene call the southern banks of the river in this valley home today, but long ago, their ancestors' settlements were routinely raided by a group of people they called the Naha, a fierce mountain-dwelling people. According to Dene lore, after the Naha had raided their camp one too many times, the Dene decided they were going to strike back. One night, the Dene made their way into the mountains to the Naha camp. When the signal was given, they attacked—but nobody was there. The Naha were nowhere to be found, neither at the camp nor in the surrounding area. Some legends say that the Naha had evaporated, turned to dust or became ghosts; others say that Dene Medicine People had turned into fierce animals so they could end the threat themselves.

The story has remained part of the mystery of Nahanni Valley ever since. When gold prospectors arrived, more tales of strange wailing winds and unexplained mists started circulating. These tales didn't dissuade the McLeod brothers, though, who sought a fortune they hoped to pluck out of the water. Family lore says the McLeods, Willie and Frank, became well known in the area; their light Scottish hair, charm and helpful hands easily identified them. Willie, rumoured to be a strong hunter, lived off the land once he arrived in Nahanni Valley. He hunted, trapped and panned for gold. In 1905, he struck gold in Bennett Creek, only to lose it when his boat capsized on his way to Fort Liard. Undaunted, he looked for more and found enough to make it worth his while to return to the fort and convince his brother, Frank, and the Scottish engineer Bobbie Weir to join him on another expedition. In 1906, they went upriver. Rumour has it that they found plenty, but the three of them were never seen alive again.

Though each legend tells it a little differently, it is said by some that in 1908 prospectors found the skeletal remains of the McLeod brothers with gunshot evidence and no trace of their third party member. The remains had been tied to trees on the bank of the Nahanni River between First and Second Canyons, and they were without their heads—which have never been found.

Who did the deed was never discovered yet suspicions arose around two men, Albert Johnson from eastern Canada and Bobbie Weir, the third missing man of the party. People in our family like to say that the man who killed the brothers went to a pub sometime after they went missing, claiming he had found gold. Whoever he was, he was never seen or heard from after that pub crawl.

In 1985, my parents bought a five-acre parcel of land on Sumas Mountain in Abbotsford, BC. The original custodians of this mountain and the valley below—what was once Sumas Lake—are the Semá:th People of the Sumas First Nation, who have lived here for over ten thousand years. While they more commonly lived closer to the area that was Sumas Lake, the mountain nonetheless housed them in times of struggle and flood. It protected them during battles and storms. It is still today a sanctuary and place of significant spiritual importance.

Sumas Mountain is central to every life within its gaze—past, present and future. Today, it is the pride and joy of the City of Abbotsford. It is a recreational playground and home to an increasing number of people. It is still the hunting grounds and ceremonial place for the Semá:th People. It is also a site for mining rock and of logging. Many of its water runs have been sold. Its land is occupied and well used—by my family as well. It is this contradiction this book honours. There is a great tendency to rewrite history, to gloss over the past, to take up space in the present and focus incessantly on the future. In these pages, I tell my story as a conflicted descendent of settlers.

It had been my parents' dream—and is likely the dream of many, though it is becoming increasingly unattainable—to buy property and build a home. They spent their first night of ownership sleeping in a tent on the eastern edge of the property next to the forest, dreaming of what this place could be. Thirty-six years later, it has become a haven for friends and family to gather.

When they purchased the property, though, only some of the land had been cleared of trees. In that clearing, they built a two-storey white house with blue trim, leftovers from that very 1980s pastel colour pallet. My mother tells the story of keeping my older brother enclosed in a playpen on the back deck while Dad and anyone who would lend a hand framed and finished the house. Next, a field was to be cleared and some fill brought in to raise the land to accommodate horses. There is a photograph of my twenty-something father in their home: thick black hair, a blue plaid jacket, dirty gloves and soot covering every inch of his wide, smiling face as a fire blazes in the background, devouring the stumps remaining on the property, remnants of old-growth logging days, along with new trees my family cleared.

To accommodate my mother's first love (horses), new neighbours—all around the same age as my parents, also with young kids, who bought land on our street at the same time—came around one afternoon for a barn raising. Mom slapped blue paint across plywood boards as the team of men measured and planned and hammered. *One, two, three, hoist*— up the walls went all at once. Then, freshly painted plywood went on next, then a roof and suddenly a gambrel-roof barn was born. Several years later, in an attempt to correct one of my teenage behaviours, my parents tasked me with re-painting this barn red. Many years after that, after leaving the property to venture into my own life, I returned and renovated the loft of the barn into a living space. From there, in the old hay storage, looking out into the forest where my parents spent their first night as landowning settlers, I have written this story.

In the 1920s, and again in the sixties, this piece of property and most of Sumas Mountain was logged. In the early eighties, my street was cleared and a road was put in. Charlie Spruce Place runs south of Dawson Road, which branches east and west from Sumas Mountain Road, the original trail that led from the north side of Sumas Mountain at the Fraser River, over the top and down to the south side and what was once Sumas Lake. The owner of the land, Charlie Spruce— his ownership the result of several generations of colonization in the Fraser Valley—had dreamed of subdividing and selling. He never lived to see this happen, but his wife did. My parents were among the first to buy here, and since then the property has raised kids and horses and dogs and goats and chickens and, yes, even the adults.

Today, our property, lined with the white fences erected by our neighbours and the edge of a forest far older than any of us, holds the remnants of an old-growth stump that protrudes out of a cleared field with a stream running through it. The house my parents built still stands on a little knoll on the north side of the property; recently, they added a rental unit on top of the garage, which houses a young couple and their toddler. The barn, where I live now, is still the home of three horses on the ground floor. Surrounding it all is the forest of Sumas Mountain and its many trails where I wander.

Gold, greed and the fallacy of progress does strange things to people. My family is not exempt from this. We have reached out and taken. We have participated in the colonization of this land and therefore the severing of the traditional and sacred relationship between humans and nature. I work every day to do better, to show respect for what we have and to cultivate connection and relationship with nature. For me, it's the only path forward.

SPRING

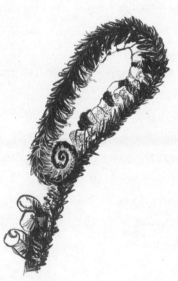

Nature's first green is gold,

Her hardest hue to hold.

Her early leaf's a flower;

But only so an hour.

Then leaf subsides to leaf.

So Eden sank to grief,

So dawn goes down to day.

Nothing gold can stay.

— "Nothing Gold Can Stay," Robert Frost (1923)

FIDDLEHEADS AND THIMBLEBERRIES

Transparent golden rays from the early sun arc over the canopy, slowly warming the lightly frosted earth. A pair of owls call out to each other in yearning. Barely audible at first, the *hoo hoo* from one owl to the next, louder then softer, reaches me in the quiet moment between sleeping and waking. The sound becomes, to my sleepy mind, a trace of something nearly forgotten and on the verge of being erased. Then I am awake. I decided in those early hours, as I so often do, to take a walk in the woods. There is fresh oxygen awaiting me on the trail.

With eyes still half open, I slip on an old pair of Merrells, brown-stained and dirty in some places and desperately faded in others. I slide open the set of glass doors at the back of my house. As if in a dream, I step onto a red-brick patio with thick spaces between each block that have been newly taken over by green and yellow spring moss. With a cool breeze tickling my neck and the shy morning casting slim rays of warmth—a promise of more spring days ahead—I exist within that great transition from winter to summer: those special days not too cold nor too hot when I have a chance to pause and feel the best of both seasons. The pandemic of 2020 has begun to loosen its tight hold on our lives and the coldest winter days are behind us. It is April 2021 and I am excited at the beginning signs of spring—new life, bright flowers and long, slow walks in the sunshine without a worry to cross my path. This resurgence gives me hope for a bright year.

My toque snug on my head and gloves tucked into my jacket pocket should I need them, I head east across the woodsy lawn grown with moss, clover and the first signs of yellow dandelions strewn haphazardly among the remnants of winter debris—fallen branches, patches of browned leftover snow and frosty earth where the sun has not yet touched. I edge behind the shed, filled with enough fir, cedar and walnut to heat our house for at least five years, and step onto the overgrown logging road. One edge, set against the rise of the mountain, is unnaturally cut into the earth; the other blends easily into the downward slope. Between the two road edges is a flat walkway, too flat to be a natural forest floor. Although trees and foliage have filled in this old road over the years, close observation will tell you there is nothing natural about it.

I walk down the reclaimed scar for a few metres, then step onto an old deer trail and into the woods. The lush West Coast rainforest of Sumas Mountain closes in around me, erasing all visible traces of humanity and replacing them with the low vibration of forest life.

It's peaceful beneath the canopy; tranquil and unassuming. A deep belly breath brings the dewy morning air that follows a rainy night into my system; I am drunk on the freshness. It permeates my bloodstream, running up and down the meridians of my body, forcing sensory reflexes to awaken. I am attentive to a complete body and mind shift that only this place provides me. I feel taller yet less imposing. I feel wider yet nimble and light. I am utterly expansive as I tune into the rhythm of the forest. My skin tingles with goosebumps, tiny hairs stand up at the back of my neck, my head grows slightly fuzzy and my limbs move into a realm of weightlessness. I am carried along by some unseen army of forest elves, beckoning me to experience spring on Sumas Mountain.

Weaving along, up and down tilted hills, my Merrells step amid last season's dormant deep-green ferns over fallen logs and around low-hanging branches. I feel as though the thrum of my heart beats with the pace of the woods. Along the trail's edges, fresh greenery is showing the first signs of budding; soon, there will be fiddleheads popping up and great bursts of salmon and thimble berries—a combination of red and yellow, fuzzy and smooth. I'll share their sweet and tangy flavour with the birds and bears, careful not to take more than my share.

I am conscious of not wanting to disturb this place any more than I need to, especially during the crucial growing months of early spring. Aware of my presence as an interloper in such a complex ecosystem, much of which I am only beginning to understand, I feel the presence of the mountain. I know I am a burden, yet despite that I feel this place open up to me. Here, I feel welcome. Here, I work through the challenging nature of this life. I am grateful.

I slowly advance among unfurling sword, lady and deer ferns. I pass tiny bleeding hearts, whose deep fuchsia will soon turn a pale blush colour as the season continues; no bigger than the nail on my pinkie finger, the early risers are only just peppering the forest floor, their heads bowed in reverie. Busy chitter chatter pulls my eye upward to search for the northern flicker woodpecker or chickadee, or the owls that woke me that morning. My ears perk up, hearing something resembling the *tap-tap-tap* of the pointy red-headed bird somewhere in the distance. My eyes search in yearning, but I never find her.

I become lost in thought, but a slight downhill curve and a recurring seasonal mushroom patch to the side of the trail, months yet to go before its return, brings my attention back to the path and then to a hand-laid bridge stretching over a wide gurgling creek. The creek is crowded, the water rushing down the mountain and away from its source farther north. Pausing here, I take a long, sweet breath. In through the nose, out through the mouth. *Whoosh.* Inhaling the slight misty air of the babbling brook as I stand among the busy beaks of local warblers and the bushy tails of squirrels, I feel, for a moment, like part of the woods. I bring myself closer to the earth, crouching beneath long, slender hemlocks shivering in the slight breeze, quietly whispering, I like to imagine, to each other about last night's secrets. I am thankful for their counsel. I can feel the forest glistening as each ray of morning light filters through the nearly translucent greenery. It is springtime on Sumas Mountain.

If I remain still long enough on that creek bank,

memories of my past come rushing back to me. I can see myself as a small girl dashing through the trees: I am a mountain goat, then a forest nymph. I am one with the woods, a woodland fairy fiercely loving and defending the wonder of this place. I am Titania in Shakespeare's *A Midsummer Night's Dream*. In one moment, I see my father, dressed in torn plaid and well-worn boots, collecting wood from a tree blown over in a recent storm. In the next moment, he is bent over a mushroom with me as we inspect its gills. We walk down the path as he tells tall tales filled with half-truths.

I hear my mother's voice, warm and calm, teaching me that we are guests in the forest and that we must be as minimally invasive as possible. "We need to leave the frogs where they sit," my mother told me when I tried, years ago, to bring one home to add to our pond. "If a frog wants to live in our pond, that's her choice. But we do not get to displace her just because it suits us," she said. I learn how to explore and play and experience all that this beautiful place presents.

I imagine remnants of these lessons in the landscape around me. Is that frog creaking in the water the great-grand-child of the one I once picked up? Is that stone in the creek the same one I hopped on at six years old, learning to cross the water without getting wet? Is that stump the same one that has been rotting for years, changing its shape over time naturally but also because I peeled at its dying bark?

The teasing laugh of a red squirrel brings me back to the present moment. I choose not to use the bridge and instead hop lightly along a line of rocks sticking up from the water's surface.

This creek has changed so much in my lifetime alone. Hopping from one stone to the next, I know they are likely not the same ones I stepped upon as a child and with my friends. I laugh, remembering how someone always slipped, unharmed, into the cold mountain water. The width of the creek has grown, then shrunk, then grown once more in response to dry summers and wet winters. There have been several forms of bridges at this creek over the years too. The first was narrow, constructed in a way that only one person could cross at a time and with extreme care. It was almost safer to gingerly step along the rocks below. In time, however, my father built a wider and more sturdy bridge with iron bars and thick beams. He even built raised edges on either side and placed old roofing on the expanse of the walking zone to avoid any slipping accidents. It was strong and wide enough for horses and a tractor to cross. With the convenience of the bridge, however, came motorized quads and motorbikes. We created the circumstances for them to play here too.

On some walks, I cannot deny that I become so preoccupied by the deep divots in the muck made by motorized tires that I forget the forest around me that I had come to enjoy. Sometimes, I hear only the echoing growl of the gravel mine in the distance, drowning out the pulse of the woods. A fearful query began to haunt me as I wondered with each walk: What new assault on the senses will I experience today? When will it ever be quiet and still again?

Continuing my wander, away from the changed creek and farther into the forest, I come to a three-pronged fork in the path marked by a tall, serrated stump. There are jagged spikes coming out of the trunk where the branches once were, suggesting the logger's tool of choice may have been a dull handheld hatchet. To the right of the stump, I notice a small white plastic bag tied up neatly and tossed alongside the trail. A printed outline of a smiling dog is just visible from where I stand. I pick up the bag and carry it home with me to the trash.

❦

When spring arrives on Sumas Mountain, carpets of ferns and flowers populate the forest floors. On days like these, I like to take an alternate route on the mountain. This path meanders around the original loop, then takes off toward the south side of the mountain, down a hill, along a ravine, across another section of the same creek I usually cross, up a hill, through an old farm now overtaken by blackberries and out through our neighbour's collection of trees. In one area along this route, where an old cutblock has been given the liberty to grow back naturally, there is an expansive patch of bleeding hearts. It feels nearly endless—and there are white trilliums among them, here and there, like large diamonds amidst the golden-green leaves and purple flowers. Robert Frost wrote that "nature's first green is gold," and here, in this magical place among the firs and cedars and poplars and alders, he's right. The blue sky casts down a spring light that makes the green shimmer like gold, but there are rubies, sapphires and diamonds too.

Standing in the patch that day, I was struck by the memory of something my dad once told me. We were on a walk on the mountain headed to this area, chatting about the weather, the world, our lives. We walked down a large hill and across a fallen tree spanning the width of the creek, used as a bridge in this part of the woods. When we approached the clearing of bleeding hearts, he tells me he saw a plant like it for sale in a shop not too long ago. "Six dollars for one bobbling pink heart, bowed over at the top," he said. Then, gesturing out to the flowers ahead of him, added, "I'm a millionaire!"

His gaze met mine and his tone shifted. "Of course, I could only be a millionaire if those plants remain in the ground. I'm rich when I have the privilege to walk among them."

SILK

When I walk early in the woods, or sometimes in the fading hours of the evening, the angle of the light allows me to see the sparkle of spiderwebs with silken strings stretched across wide and narrow places along the trail behind my house. If I can catch a glimpse of silk before walking into it, I gently dismantle one corner attached to a leaf or branch or bush so I can pass through. If possible, I will duck under or step over or around the web, so carefully crafted in the way only a spider can spin. I do what I can to avoid destroying the snare the small spider hiding nearby has set up to catch her next meal. If such destruction is unavoidable, as sometimes the light hits the silken web in just the right way to make the trap invisible, I apologize to her for tearing open her intricate, delicate weave, so often recognized as creepy.

Is it possible to cultivate empathy for the nonhuman? Can I have empathy for a creek in the same way that I empathize with spiders? I ask myself these questions out loud as I step around that beautifully intricate web, contorting my body into a surrealist painting so as not to disturb the large silk reaching across the width of the trail at chest height, about four feet off the ground. I often speak out loud when I walk here. I feel comfortable doing this not because the trees don't speak back, for they do communicate with each other and with me in their own way, but because I feel they may have the answers I am looking for, if only I give them the time and stillness they require to provide those answers.

As I correct my body into a more human position, I hear the huff of our old springer spaniel, Charlie, down the trail. She's slower than she used to be and is often left behind to sleep on patio furniture on our front porch. Today, though, it appears she woke up, caught a scent and refused to be left behind. I wait for her on the other side of the spider's silk as the panting grows nearer and Charlie rounds the corner in the distance—ears flopping, legs racing, her brown and white coat jiggling a little more than in her youth, mouth hanging open and tongue nearly dragging on the forest floor. Her eyes glisten with joy as I beckon her into my arms. She races beneath the spider web without even considering the possibility of its existence and licks my face as I bend down to meet her.

When I look into Charlie's eyes, I always feel as if she knows what I'm feeling. When I'm sad, she softens and comforts. When I'm excited, she mirrors that mood with an entire body wag. If I'm afraid of some unseen threat, she stands at attention, ready to protect. And I do the same for her.

Charlie and I continue through the woods, slower together but happy. Charlie bulldozes her way through bushes along the side of the path I walk on, destroying every spider web in her way. By the time we make it home, the white of her feet have turned brown, leaves are stuck to her tail and in the low-hanging fur on her belly, and her face is covered in silky webs.

SWALLOWS

Barn swallows—the acrobats of the sky, who soar and tumble and dodge to impressively catch flies—migrate to and from Sumas Mountain every spring and fall. Every April, I anxiously await their arrival. They make their way up from Mexico and Central America using the Pacific Flyway; one or two will arrive on our property first, and then larger groups follow. They return to nests in the rafters of our barn—nests left behind by their ancestors, year after year, which each new arrival revitalizes with fresh horsehair and moss to signify that it's occupied.

Their day begins, bright and early, loud and boisterous, each morning. Sleeping above them in a renovated loft, I hear them twitter and chirp, warble and cry, from when the sky starts to lighten until the sun peeks through the trees—which is when the show of acrobatic flight commences. Sometimes, they will quiet down momentarily, but they will start up again as soon as a single bird chirps. Soon, everyone has an opinion—on what exactly I am unsure. The floorboards of my loft ignite with dynamic swallow gossip, marking the beginning of mating season. I look forward to feeling their energy all year, and I like to anticipate what I might learn from their interactions with each other and with the space they occupy in the sky.

While I know the abundant noise is part of their mating ritual, I like to imagine that they might be communicating about their long trip up the Pacific Flyway. I wonder, too, how that migratory route may have been negatively impacted by human intervention. Was a crucial resting ground along the way newly developed? Did they eat insects tarnished by pesticides?

Not long after their flurry of arrival, I begin to spot anywhere between three and eight small white eggs with reddish brown spots and flecks in most nests. At this point, the early morning gab sessions grow quieter and less frequent. The days grow longer; at dusk they dance triumphantly, tumbling to snatch up mosquitoes and flies while nearly colliding with one another, playing a talented game of chicken yet knowing precisely where and how fast their wingspan can take them.

When the nestlings hatch, the chattering starts up again at dawn, loud and clear. I lay in bed and note the difference: now, the mature call of the parent is punctuated by the desperation of their hungry young. I love to go into the barn and spy on the tiny heads peeking out of fluffy nests. The parents, already up and searching for food, come and go. Those resting near the ceiling turn their heads in my direction when I walk in. They *cheep, cheep, cheep* with excitement or alarm, then cast off and out into the open air. They know every inch of the barn—where the openings are, where their nest is, which wire or post or stall edge they can land on.

Some days, when it's been too cold or too hot or the population of bugs is unseasonably low, the swallows are very quiet when I enter the barn. I know what this means. I walk through and check the floors of each stall. In one of them I will find an emaciated chick alone and lifeless. Opening the stall door, I bend down to scoop up the body. The bird's head may wobble to one side, but the body is already stiff. It feels weightless in my hands, no bigger than the head of a tulip, as I take it out to the trees and say goodbye.

Those at the South Coast Conservation Program and Fraser Valley Conservancy don't always know for certain what causes a bird's death. A myriad of reasons could be the answer and a combination is likely. Some claim heavy pesticide use can wipe out the insect population or poison the birds who eat the infected bugs, which can be lethal or impact successful reproduction and healthy nestlings. The way this pollution is passed through species is aptly named secondary poisoning, and it highlights how vulnerable ecosystems can be when even a single element is tampered with.

Others suggest that the decreasing number of barn swallows is also due to the demolition of barns and other man-made structures or habitats. When these structures are torn down, the migratory birds must nest elsewhere quickly, often building them in dangerous or unstable areas. When the bird population grows smaller, the insect population grows larger. The greater the swarms of insects, the more difficult it is to manage bug populations; this is hard on the farmers who grow our local produce, which can often lead to the use of pesticides. The more we spray, the more birds eat infected bugs and the more we will find the scattered bodies of lifeless birds.

On a spring night one June, I hosted an outdoor dinner party for friends and family. We were sitting out on the grass in the backyard; we sipped on glasses of Riesling underneath strings of warm lights. We sat around the candlelit table in wide-seated, reclaimed teak chairs, dishes at each place setting scraped clean, as we chatted about our lives and memories and the dreams we had yet to realize. The evening air was warm and the stars began to glow when one among us remarked at how few bugs were flitting about. We nostalgically discussed dragonflies, once a staple in the skies as the air warmed each year; their transparent, rainbow-tinted wings seemed to catch and refract each ray of sunshine and their otherworldly, mermaid-like bodies were beautiful in their alterity. They were expert dancers, and I would watch as one rested on a blade of grass, tilting it over ever so slightly, before taking off once again to continue its choreography elsewhere as the last golden rays of the day retreated.

I told my friends about moths the size of small maple leaves that used to come out after dusk throughout my childhood. When the back porch light went on, they would collect there, glued to the glow of the glass encasing the light fixture, sharing the space with other moths of many sizes, shapes and colours. I remember watching them flutter and rest, flutter and rest, in one moment completely manic and in the next part of a well-painted tapestry. There were also ladybugs, the nine-spot and two spot-breeds, whose ability to expansively populate our south-facing kitchen window became an elaborate game between six-year-old me and them, where I tried to anticipate where they were going with such a dedicated march. In the grass, too, those red and black ladies seemed to be everywhere. They crawled on my hands and arms and along my toes and in the curves of my feet. Once they were on me, I laid still so as not to disturb their determination. They certainly had somewhere to go—or perhaps it really was nowhere, for they seemed to me to wander here and there endlessly. These days, as foreign breeds take over, I am lucky to spot a handful of the native ladybug all season.

As we discussed our bug tales that June evening, we noticed a mosquito buzzing among us from one person to the next, hovering before each of our faces. We watched but we did not move; nobody raised a hand to swat her away.

I once heard a radio interview with neuroscientist Vivek Jayaraman who was talking about the wonder of fruit flies. As we watched the mosquito glide among us, I retold the story to my friends. Since 2014, Jayaraman's Virginia-based team and researchers at Google have been mapping the brain of the fruit fly. They discovered that there was more going on in these small brains than most of us realize: in one section, there is a complex circuitry that informs the fly whether it has eaten enough, where its next meal might be located in the vicinity and where it's located in space at all times—which could explain, I suppose, why the fly always makes a B-line for my expensive red wine over a browning banana on the counter. Apparently, the fly never forgets where it is, how it got there and what it's intended purpose was in entering my home.

As I finished the story, we watched as the mosquito hovered among us, lingering for several minutes, and then floated upwards, to where I knew swallows would soon be ending their daily flight and vacating the area to make way for a collection of little brown bats. Whatever her fate that evening, my friends and I decided to let this mosquito go. She was free from our quick hands and irritation. At that moment, we saw the mosquito differently. We decided to appreciate the complex systems that make up even the most seemingly inconsequential and irritating creatures.

THE VOICE OF NATURE

The voice of nature—its elusive whispers, ghostly howls, quiet winds, silent movements. I believe that I have heard it a few times in my life. It speaks not in words that people have invented, but in moods that frighten and inspire, that soothe and calm and bring clarity to the mind. I have troubles hearing it in the summer and winter: in the summer the mountain and its inhabitants roar to life and there is too much activity; in the winter, life is hard and I have troubles silencing the dialogue in my mind. But I have heard it during the crisp mornings of fall and golden-sunset evenings of spring, where silence opens offerings of transformation. When the mountain is shifting from season to season there is a pause, an opening, and there I have heard the quieted voice of nature so often overpowered. There is an opportunity for openness at the moment of transition, as trees grow airy and spacious or flourish and fill in. These in-between days, before the foliage is at its sparsest or fullest, is when the voice of nature speaks the loudest.

When the rain rushes in with spring, heavy drops pound my tin roof and sound like the clattering of blue marbles in a glass jar that I have just shaken. During the windy

April storms of recent years, long icy fingers reach into the cracks of the barn, heave at the edges of my home with all their might, creeping into nooks and crannies of the siding, pulling at the seams and rushing down the building's frame, attempting to relieve the tin from its shackles. On nights like these, unable to sleep without vivid dreams of roaring creatures, I lay and listen, half-petrified and half-stunned with awe at the power of that wind.

My senses come alive. I open the windows fully and draw up the blinds to let the wet, warm spring air carry moisture into my sleeping space. It hangs heavy in the atmosphere and rustles the large, weighty map of the world—long out of date—I hung up on the wall many years ago. The wooden dowel attached to the map and secured to the wall keeps the world straight but *tap-tap-taps* on the wall with each flick of air. There is nothing to do but listen and feel the weather. I climb back into bed, safe and warm cocooned in blankets and pillows, and I stare into the textured darkness that the open window has brought inside. I sense Wind move around my space like an entity alive and breathing. Outside, solar lights are triggered by large, wet drops, which send sporadic shadows of trees and leaves to pattern the walls of my white shiplap bedroom. A heavy-scented dew reaches me along a trail of rain-traced air; a strong, deep inhale transports my memory to other times and places where rain and nature's voice worked their magic on me once before.

In the Sichuan province of Central China, Mount Emei rises three thousand metres into the clouds. As the highest of four sacred mountains, Mount Emei, sitting at the western rim of the province, is an anchor of wisdom. One year, after staying a night at the bottom of the mountain, A. and I, without much planning or preparation, began hiking to the 3,099-metre summit.

The trail begins by passing through lush forest, namely made up of Faber fir, or *abies fabri,* a rare and threatened species unique for their foliage arrangement. The trees were teeming with thieving Tibetan macaques. Their eyes followed us as they looked for an opportunity to rummage through our packs. Evidence of their conquests littered the path and forest: chip bags, eggshells, water bottles and empty plastic vessels, all their contents long gone, were everywhere. Luckily, we had nothing these creatures wanted and they left us alone as we continued on our way.

By the time A. and I had been hiking for several hours, we still had not reached the golden temple at the top. Nightfall was approaching quickly. We cursed our lack of preparedness. What began as a last-minute decision to hike to the peak became a desperate push against the quickening of night to reach another temple closer to us. Soon, we were hiking in the dark, barely able to see where to place each step on the stone path leading us upward. Our knowledge of the route was seriously lacking and our sense of foolishness growing.

Suddenly, the skies unloaded a heavy and continuous rain. There were no lights to lead our way up the narrow, steep, slippery stone steps, but we had no choice but to precariously hike into the night. We ascended extremely slowly, grasping slippery trees at the sides of the trail for guidance.

My legs had turned to lead and, cold, afraid, and frustrated at my own stupidity, a sense of dread overwhelmed me. We were becoming increasingly desperate and knew we needed to get to our destination fast. The rain was relentlessly pounding against my body and every inch of my clothes was soaked. A. went ahead and around a corner while I slowed down and soon stopped stepping forward altogether. As I rested, I looked up and closed my eyes, feeling the sky's water heavy on my face, and wondered how I could have been so careless.

Realizing the possible severity of my situation, I cried—fat, ridiculous sobs. I wondered what they would say when they found the body of a Canadian who had become lost on one of the most popular trails in China. I felt as if my knees might buckle under the weight of my own shame. My shoulders leaned into soft moss lining the rocky side of the mountain, feeling ready for it to swallow me whole.

Then, as if someone had turned off a faucet, the rain suddenly stopped. In disbelief, I looked up and around to see if I had imagined it. The rain, I decided, had indeed stopped, for as I glanced to my right, away from where I leaned, I didn't see raindrops but instead saw a small speck of light floating in the trees. Transfixed, I stared. The entity glowed for a moment, suspended, then drifted toward me and hovered a few inches from my face. Then, it continued in the direction of the mountain path. My gaze remained fixed upon it. When I took a small step forward toward the light, the entire mountain lit up with thousands of fireflies illuminating the road before me.

Enchanted, I started hiking again. Almost in a trance, the lights pulled me forward. They led me around a corner and up a steep incline. For the remainder of the hike, time was immeasurable.

At some point, off in the distance and atop a small hill, as if it had been born out of the mist, were the lights of a temple. A. was standing in front of it, waving her arms frantically in my direction. The sight took my breath away. The temple glowed, beckoning me toward it. The warm yellow light flowing out from the windows shone on the stone ground surrounding the building—the recently ended rainfall had everything sparkling. I turned around for one last look at the path and saw the fireflies retreating to the forest. Then, modest and indifferent as it always is, the forest carried on with its own business.

PAINTED GIFTS

In late May, when yellow-headed skunk cabbage had filled the soft marshy areas of Sumas Mountain, a parade of painted rocks appeared along the trails near our house. Adorned with assorted plants, vegetables and fruits, the rocks traced the edges of trails and various crevices and corners circling our still relatively winterized neighbourhood. Nobody I spoke to seemed to know where they came from, who painted them or why. Not the multigenerational family up the street where Charlie Spruce meets Dawson Road. Not the other multigenerational family who lives down the road, up the hill and at the beginning of the cul-de-sac in their 1980s log home. Not even the little girl who lives with her family at the bottom of that same dead-end road, who rides her purple bike and plays in the creek behind her house, nearby the same trail decorated with those mysterious painted rocks.

Everyone on our street has access to these trails one way or another. Many have built their own narrow access points from their backyards to join the growing web of networks leading from one end of Charlie Spruce Place to the other, looping behind the acreage of each resident. At the start of the pandemic, those trails were traipsed upon more frequently than ever before. It was a regular occurrence to be wandering in the forest at any point in the day and come across a neighbour who was doing precisely the same as me: escaping the confines of their home to take a walk in the woods. Over a year into the pandemic, once the world tentatively reopened and we returned to our offices, the trails grew quieter in the day. So, when I took my daily walk in the afternoons and those rocks suddenly appeared, nobody knew who painted them. A wonderful mystery was born.

For weeks, a new masterpiece would pop up each day. On Monday, an orange carrot in the crevice of a cedar, complete with black lines to show the carrot's tiny creases. A brown-spotted mushroom nestled at the base of a decaying stump by the following Friday. Soon, an eggplant, a tomato, an apple, a sweet onion, a few more carrots, a purple flower and a red, spotted ladybug also became part of the landscape. By early June, a second or third or fourth rendition of each vegetable had appeared on differently sized and shaped rocks but no bigger than the palm of my hand. One lonely strawberry graced the corners of the forest.

I anticipated a new painted stone each walk I took that spring—a small joy in a difficult world. Although the frequency of their appearance slowed over time, by that summer's end, the trails were filled with them. I felt, despite the mystery of who painted and placed the stones, more connected to my community and to the woods, as if we were all speaking a common language without using any words at all. It felt wonderful to be seen without being seen—a small token of passive kindred acknowledgement.

As parts of the world continued to reopen once pandemic restrictions eased, more rock paintings failed to appear and I still had not encountered the artist. I mourned the absence of the broccoli, lettuce and beet. I wondered why edible native plant species—stinging nettle, wild roses, blackberries, Indian plums, dandelion flowers, devil's club—didn't make the artist's cut. But whoever it was and whatever the reason, I saw it as someone creatively connecting with the forest, and I in turn was connecting with them. By observing the paths and meandering slowly enough to find just the right spot to place a carrot, one might see the forest changing and breathing and living day to day.

The gift of these stones—almost indiscernible, hidden among the trees and not obtusely placed along the path, left to fade and disappear into the growing landscape throughout the season—led me to believe the artist likely understood the magic of this place, likely connected to it. They, too, may strive to see this place in all its fullness and individuality.

OPHELIA

A strange light greets me in the forest. Distant whispers I'm unable to comprehend trace the centre of my mind—but I know what they are saying. I know because of the feelings and sensations they give me. I am seeing without seeing, moving without moving, existing as myself but not as myself as I walk barefoot in a wooded area, much like the forest behind my home on Sumas Mountain. I walk among the trees and mosses and leaves, stepping over root systems, around lady ferns and sword ferns and along the soft lichen thick ground made up of new spring shoots and the remnants of winter decay. I feel the earth breathe beneath me, with me, as me, and the pulse of my heart radiates through and entwines with the pulse of the earth. One heartbeat. Heel-toe, heel-toe; I walk with arms soft and calm at my sides, my legs effortlessly carrying me along, my body light yet grounded. As if I know what comes next, I glance to my right and smile. There, walking alongside me, is a wolf with a white-and-silver-streaked coat and eyes bluer than any blue I have ever known. They hold the ocean of the earth and the depth of the sky, the past, present and future. I look into her sharp gaze and, as she stares back at me, I become her.

I continue to walk, with the awareness that I am beside myself simultaneously in wolf and human form. These dual forms of me periodically glance at one another and I shift consciousnesses and perspective with each turn of the eye. We continue this way until a bend in the trail reveals a deep, wide, yet slow-moving stream. We cease our steps simultaneously, exchanging looks. I become the wolf and the human, transferring identities with ease until finally my human form is floating downstream. I become my human form singularly, face toward the sky, arms and legs stretched out ever so lightly, hair billowing around me as it takes on the wetness of the water. I am Ophelia singing. I am drowning, like Ophelia, but not dying. I have lost my rational mind but found something much better, more connected. I am becoming the water and the rocks and sand beneath—an end that sparks a new beginning.

An extreme sense of calm washes over me as I glide downstream. Along the shoreline, the wolf follows, watching me as I watch her. I feel the earth breathing in the pulse of the creek and the movement of the air, the steps of the wolf and the weightlessness of the human. One heartbeat. I take it all in, becoming part of it all. Every molecule of each living thing is me and I am it, simultaneously human, wolf, water, air and earth.

I never reach the end of the stream in this dream. I always wake somewhere gliding in the water. Perhaps there is no end. In waking, I feel an incredible sense of calm and ease, the same sensation I felt with the fireflies on Mount Emei. I know I am a part of everything and everything is a part of me.

This recurring dream first began when I was sixteen and I always had it in the spring. It is always the same, with identical beings and storyline, but it arrives for different reasons, and I wake with a different perspective each time it comes.

The dream came back nightly in the beginning, then weekly, then monthly, until it ceased for some time. Now I have it when life's challenges compound, but whether or not I've had it recently, I can always return to the impact it's had on my consciousness. The dream has shaped the way I exist and how I interact with this planet. This I know is how Nature speaks to me.

SUMMER

And only where the forest fires have sped,

Scorching relentlessly the cool north lands,

A sweet wild flower lifts its purple head,

And, like some gentle spirit sorrow-fed,

It hides the scars with almost human hands.

And only to the heart that knows of grief,

Of desolating fire, of human pain,

There comes some purifying sweet belief,

Some fellow-feeling beautiful, if brief.

And life revives, and blossoms once again.

— "Fire-Flowers," E. Pauline Johnson (1894)

Mountain Serenade

Summer on Sumas Mountain is the closest to paradise as
I have ever known. The forest, a deep and varied landscape of emerald, olive and sage, sings with the abundance of
life. Bees bustle around pollinating and barn swallows have
taught their babies to soar by the spring's end, so now they
swoop and tumble through the air together like nature's original acrobats. I savour food from our backyard garden and
smell the sweet aroma of wild Nootka roses along forest trails.
Sometimes, I intently scour the forest floor for the vanilla
leaf, whose scent is light—much stronger when dried—but
a necessary addition to these olfactory summer moments in
the woods. Sumas Mountain's atmosphere in the summer has a
fullness that only a temperate rainforest can produce. Even the
assault of the nearby gravel mine or the clearing of trees and
onset of new construction that comes with summer is muted
by the cacophony of warbly birds, summer storms, long hours
of warm sunlight and a forest that breathes greenery into every
molecule of my body. At least—I am productively, if only momentarily, distracted by these events of summer.

This was my state of mind as I got myself ready one early summer morning to hike up to Chadsey Lake. There are a

few ways to get to the lake, but I always choose the same one: the 10.5-kilometre out-and-back centennial trail, originally built in 1967.

I awoke early when the sun was just beginning to slide up into the sky. I climbed into my Chevrolet Bolt and drove the couple kilometres to the trailhead with the windows rolled all the way down. I parked on the gravel road on the north side of the mountain and began my walk alone. Passing through the trailhead threshold and past the sign warning of bears and wildlife, I strapped a dangling red bear bell to my pack so as not to spook an unsuspecting creature who might be drinking or cooling themselves at one of the many creeks I pass over. It was early but warm, so I wore quick-dry hiking shorts and an old Vancouver Sun Run T-shirt, a Tilley hat and sunblock and, aside from a water bottle and some snacks, took very little else with me.

I kick up dust as I walk down the first stretch of the path. Tall cedars with drooping boughs hang down all around me. I come to Wade's Creek—the first body of water to pass, only a few feet wide and moving slowly with the summer trickle—and cross the wooden bridge that spans it. On the other side, the path goes uphill. I follow it and begin to sweat as the summer heat grows with the inclining sun. My body is working hard to continue a fast pace.

If I don't stop along the way, this route will take me just under two hours to reach the lake. But it is hot today, so when I come across one of the many unnamed creeks the path passes over, I linger for a bit. I crouch down and stick my fingers in the cool water, just to feel it flow around and over my hands. A kiss from the earth. I breathe the moving air, touched by moisture in these low-lying areas, look around the forest and remain still while I cool off slightly. I listen to the movement of the trees. A raven purrs quietly to no one somewhere nearby and the water bubbles and trickles on its way downhill. With hands still submerged, I turn them over to form a cup with my palms then raise them to meet my lips. Water cascades over the edges of this temporary vessel as I quickly drink the sweet mountain water. It cools my rising body temperature on this warm day, and I feel ready to continue toward the lake.

My goal is to get to the lake and take a swim before I encounter any other person, but I know that a different path comes from a parking lot farther into the mountain and many hikers will start their walk there. But there is no one with me now, so I get to walk at my own pace with my own thoughts. As the sun continues to rise higher, ever-changing light casts new shadows on the varied greenery of the forest. Light filters gently through the needles of the pines and firs, illuminates the cells and veins of maple leaves, casting strange and beautiful shadows onto the dry path I walk on. There is a mixture of scents surrounding me: hot dry earth, as if someone brought dirt into a sauna, and light florals, a complex combination of sappy pine needles, cedar bark, sweet vine maple and the light tangents of vanilla leaf.

About halfway to the top, part of the trail passes over a logging road. I step out of the thicket of trees to the great openness of the road and more-recently logged areas. By this point, the sun is much higher and I immediately feel the heat;

neither this ground nor I are protected by the tree cover and coolness the forest brings. I walk a few hundred metres along the road until I meet a massive fallen tree pushed aside. I stop there for a moment, take a sip of water and then head into the next section of trail. This section borders recently logged blocks and as I snake up through the forest still standing, I look out to see the vast emptiness of missing trees.

I stop when the path leads me to the edge of the forest. If I were to take a step forward, off the path, I would land on barren earth surrounded by dull red stumps. This area is not exactly freshly cut, but the lack of growth around the carcasses and the tiny, planted trees all around suggests it's not an old cut area either. In the distance, I can see a small collection of houses and the road leading up to them. I have felt happily alone walking up the trail so far, but here I remember that there are others not far away.

The warming sun bakes this desolate landscape. It's a wonder in this heat how those saplings, without a robust root system to support them, will be able to grow into a forest. How many of them will die before reaching maturity? How many will rot when the heavy rains come? I'm in a daze—wondering, watching—until a small blue flutter, no bigger than a quarter, catches my eye. A butterfly. She is hovering next to me, beating her powdery baby blue wings furiously. I watch her. Then, another quarter-sized butterfly, white, joins in the dance. They hover together. My gaze follows them as they move along in front of me and away from the cutblock into the depth of the forest where my trail continues. Where they're headed, the trees are glowing with sunlight. It's true that I mourn the forest when it falls. But there is still so much beauty here, so much life in these little pockets of resistance. I turn my back to the cutblock and continue up the path and into the woods.

Farther along, there is a marshy area just out of sight from the trail surrounded by ground cover, shrubbery and low-branching vine maples. It is quiet today, and always is when I pass through in the summer, but I can hear in my memory the deafening chorus of large Pacific treefrog gatherings. I remember the first time I heard their song. It was late spring and I was wandering up this trail, lost in my own mind, when I came across this section of the path and was forced to stop by the intensity of the sound that greeted me. The croaks of these frogs surrounded my senses: they were everywhere, chirping at different tones and volumes. I could also hear the strange, choked rubber band of the adult green frog and the stuttering of the red-legged frog. I was quite sure I could hear the low-toned bleat of the Oregon spotted frog, too, which doesn't sound much like a frog to me at all. I remember being so intensely engrossed, staring into the trees and the wet earth and marsh beyond the trail, that a hiker coming up behind me had to tap me on the shoulder and ask me if I was okay. I like it when the beauty of the natural world renders me mute, if only for a moment. I briefly recalled that moment to the present and then continued my way.

Near the last stretch of the trail there is a lookout. In the fall, this is where the temperature shifts dramatically from chilly to cold and where there is sometimes a line of snow marking where the sun is no longer reaching. But on a bright summer day, this lookout is all I need to muster up the last bit of strength to finish my hike. From the edge of the mountain, I can see the Fraser River, the Dewdney community, Dewdney Peak and Nicomen Mountain standing proud in the distance. Streaks of golden rays pass through sporadic fluffy white clouds punctuating the pure-blue sky above and illuminating the earth below. Sections of trees in the valley, the green fields and a sandbar peeking out from the surface of the Fraser River are glowing.

It is difficult for me to turn away from this sight, but a crash in the woods coming from the trail behind me suggests someone else has had the same idea as me that day. I take one last look at the valley then continue my ascent.

When I crest a small hill after a long, precarious and narrow section of trail and see the steep, sloped path coming downward from the trailhead farther up the mountain, I know the lake is just around the corner. I pick up my pace—heel-toe, heel-toe—round a bend, slip through a thicket of small Douglas firs and, finally, I am standing before the glistening surface of Chadsey Lake. The sun is just at the right height for the surface to sparkle as it moves with the wind or by the force of unseen creatures and currents in the darkness below. I watch the water move for a short time until the hiker on my heels catches up. We nod to one another with gentle smiles. He leaves me be and continues the route that will take him either around the circumference of the lake and back to the trail we'd both arrived on, or he will take the trail that leads to that sweeping view at the very top. I watch him leave, then return my gaze to the splendour before me.

The little island in the middle of the lake, covered with smaller trees, beckons to me. I want to swim out to meet it and sit on the rocks along its edge and enjoy the peace of existing on my own private little island. I take a long, indulgent drink of water, devour a handful of dates, slip off my boots, socks and pack and hang them in a nearby tree, and edge toward the skirt of the lake. The water near this fringe is deep enough for a shallow dive and I jump in—arms forward, legs straight, head tucked in.

I am instantly cooled. The fresh water has been slightly warmed by the summer weather and I am encased in what feels like silk. After only a moment under water, I swim to the surface. My eyelashes are wet and I spin slowly, egg beating in a full circle, to take in the full lakeshore dotted with Douglas firs. The sky above has been cleared of clouds and all I see is an expanse of blue curling down to touch the edges of the tree canopy. I slip my head under water again, eyes shut tightly, and blow bubbles back up to the surface. Then I begin to swim to the island.

I am not a fast swimmer and take many breaks to turn onto my back and gaze into the sky. When I reach the island after about five minutes of swimming leisurely, I climb onto the rocky edge and rest. The lake, hugged by trees, shines. The sun is high in the sky now and the summer heat is coming in fast, and on this little island I have a chance to enjoy it all—the occasional chirping chickadee, thick ripples from small fish that nibble at bugs resting on the lake surface, that slight breeze that always seems to be here as if it's the breath of the mountain, warmth from the sun and a wide-open sky—a beautiful fullness that only nature can create, that only Sumas Mountain can create in its own unique way. As I sit there, taking it all in, the world—just for that moment—is perfect.

FOREST BATHING

In the middle of our horse field sits a large rock. Plopped at the east end of a row of fruit trees—plum, cherry, apple, pear and fig—the rock has proven to be an ideal location to sit and watch the world. When I sit on this stone, with its flat top about four feet off the ground, I feel the earth sway around me and in me. I feel the sturdy strength of the hard rock connected to the earth and to the grasses and mosses and clover spreading out to the forest beyond. Despite the busyness of the world beyond me, when I sit here I feel a complete stillness within. The air pulses with a slight breeze, but here, where I am, breathlessness dominates.

To be still—to pause—invites seeing in the most basic sense. From this rock, I see how the wind breathes. I see it begin with the smaller young alders closest to me, then to the young orchard along the fence line, then further into the wall of greenery surrounding me. Even the biggest branches on the tallest trees quiver at the slightest wind with rhythmic tension. As the breeze rises, the forest greets it like an old friend, leaning in to scoop and carry it up, then toss it lovingly back into the sky. Once the wind passes by, the trees grow still again.

In this field, taller grasses wave their stalks, mirroring and mimicking the trees. Yellow heads of dandelions and buttercups lean and bow, bobbling back and forth, but the white clover closest to the ground is the most interesting. Nestled amid green and yellow grasses are the white pom-pom tops of clover flowers, no bigger than the nail of your thumb.

One day, sitting on my flat rock with the wind at my back, I noticed one white pom at first. I watched it closely, studying the way it bobbled in the breeze. Upon closer inspection, I discovered that the bauble-like structure is made up of white and pinkish upturned, moon-shaped petals folded slightly at the edges, concealing more layers of the same structure within; one in another and another and another held together by greenish-pink stems, its base culminating at the peak of a green stalk that connects the clover, with only three leaves rather than lucky four, to the earth.

In inspecting the white clover, I am possessed by the need to glance over the entire field. My chin rises enough for my eyes to see so many of those little white clover heads. They are everywhere. A parade of tiny cheerleaders shaking their poms in celebration of summer. Of course, they were always there. Why hadn't I noticed them before?

Pondering this new vision, a honeybee joins the conversation. She buzzes into my field of view. My eye follows her as she lands on top of the pom I had been studying, promenades in a perfect circle, then dives headfirst to mine for pollen, her bee bum in the air. When she is finished, she beats her little wings. Lift off. Hovering as if scoping out the product, she soon carries on to the next flower and the next and the next. I watch her, marvelling at her ability to carry her own weight on those ridiculously small flappers. She floats from this flower to that, lifting off and exploring another patch, circling in the air streams. I follow her movement until, as if my eyes had opened for the first time to see what was before me, the entire field comes alive with buzzing creatures.

The longer I watch the bees, the more I notice the variety of them. Large, fat bumblebees, pale-yellow-and-black-striped honeybees, small and thin mason bees, and wild bees. They are all so uniquely different. A monarch butterfly catches my eye—a rare sight these days! Then I notice some other butterflies—white, blue, yellow and black. A pair of dragonflies dance together. Was everyone there when I sat down earlier? Did I walk through a field of winged bugs to get to my stone and not notice them at all? These insects are so vital to the ecosystem on Sumas Mountain. I know how fortunate I am to be able to notice them, watch them and sit among them.

Each day I sit down there, I exist in a space where I don't need to make an argument for the value of stillness and observation. I don't need to explain to anyone why this passive wisdom I cultivate on my stone is good for my well-being and the well-being of the earth that feeds me. My senses open me up to the world directly in front of me, to what was, what is and what could be.

Just as I think I am discovering the answer to all the world's problems, a bumblebee flies directly into my forehead. Stunned, the bee immediately fusses, retreats and redirects.

To her, I had completely disappeared into the background during her quest for pollen. With this hit and skedaddle, time suddenly returns to the immediate moment. The heat of the rock beneath me pulls at my attention. I'd been sitting there long enough for morning to turn into the afternoon and the heat of summer had begun its harsh beat down. I needed to find another place to be, another contemplative spot.

As if the earth felt my stalling, a heavy wind, larger than any yet that day, rushed at me from some unknown place. The trees that had been gently swaying in the breeze creaked and bent heavily to one side, then the other. The tips of tall grasses leaned over to tickle the ground. The fruit trees rustled their broadleaf foliage. Somewhere a door left open slammed shut. I stood up, my hair and sweater caught in the sweeping spires of an invisible force, and made my way out of the field in search of another place to witness, really witness, the world. Almost in a trance, I found myself, like I so often do, headed toward the woods.

Sumas has been my prescription to nearly all that has ailed my mind and heart. It is my place for forest bathing—or *shinrin-yoku*—in any season. I especially love the scent of the woods as it exhales after a downpour, during a light rain or right before the skies turn dark and the air grows heavy. I love the singing birds as they hop from branch to branch each morning, and the silence that comes when night descends and the stars start to wink. When I brush my hand against a fern, I love its soft feathery surface. Touching the bark of trees, rough and smooth, holding the head of a trillium in my palm, and running my fingers along the surface of all kinds of moss, thick and full, thin and spiky, fills me with complete peace. This is where I go to refill my prescription.

As I wandered into the woods that day, I discovered that the water in the creek was low. I walked over to the face of the trickling waterfall. Here, mosquitos, flies, beetles and other winged insects culminated like gathering clouds before a storm. I was grateful for the slight breeze coming both through the trees and off the moving water, keeping the insects around but at bay from my bubble. The fresh water trickled past me as I climbed; it weaved its way down into the lowest crevices, settling for a moment in shallow pools dotted with water skeeters skimming the surface, and then pushing itself over the pools' edges, heading onward.

Adoring the natural rhythm of this place, I found a ledge halfway up the rock face, slid my sneakers off and placed them beside me and then settled in. I remained still and silent in this alternate grounded stone spot. My aim: to exist and connect. Green and burnt-red pine needles fluttered down from a tree along the creek's fringe above me. They flickered in the wind and afternoon sun, tumbling, descending like stardust and punctuating the point where the sunlight meets the breeze. *Forest confetti*, I think as I close my eyes. I tilt my head back, let the trimmings bounce on my cheeks and land in my hair and on my shoulders. One or two fall down the back of my loose collared blue plaid, but I don't mind. I'll shake the remnants loose on the walk home.

The stardust slows and then stops, in step with the breeze. I keep my eyes closed. I sense when the trees shift. I hear the rustle of the pine branches and then feel a needle on my nose. A streak of sunlight passes through my closed eyelids. When the visual dissipates, I become aware of other points of contact between my body and the earth. I feel wet moss in the spaces between my toes. A fern growing in the rock behind me brushes my left shoulder when a slight swivel of air encourages its movement. A bee—I am uncertain what kind, for I refuse to open my eyes—buzzes in circles above me for a moment or two before taking off. The steady trickle of water is broken up by a small *ploop* or *sploosh*. Did a cedar drop an oval cone into a shallow pool? Was a water-logged stick displaced and sent over a small ledge? Did the water suddenly surge down an alternate direction?

Shy sunlight hidden behind a tree suddenly shifts into existence with the re-settling of maple leaves in an elusive wind. Bright warmth rests on my face. Instant joy. I hear the maple trees rustling. A robin chirps, calling out in the distance. I can feel the sturdiness of the rock shelf beneath me as it keeps the trees along the perimeter of the creek standing tall, holding the earth in place and coaxing the water downward. Something crawls onto my ankle and then briskly off the other side. A plane interjects, its low drawl dominating the soundscape of the wide sky overhead for a moment. A car speeds up Dawson Road.

A gust of wind brings a gentle mist up from the water, coolly kissing my left cheek. I breathe in deeply before easily exhaling the day. Eyes still closed, I can sense light from the sun shifting again. I open each lid slowly, just in time to catch a couple pine needles fall again, to witness the shadows of maple trees cast a disco pattern onto the surface of the water below. Two white moths tumble over each other, their powdery wings at the whim of an air current I cannot see.

I gaze down at the pool beneath me. Rays of sunlight bounce on the raised borders of ripples, built and dismantled continuously by falling water. I stare, transfixed at shimmering divots of light everywhere in the liquid basin. Mesmerized. Hypnotized. Like looking into a burning flame. My attention falls heavily to these glowing orbs on the creek's surface. They multiply and grow brighter. The light is their energy source. As my eyes slightly defocus, the smaller points of lights merge, forming one massive shimmering body of water. I am enraptured by it, and I am still aware of falling pine needles, buzzing flies and mosquitoes, scuttling bronze ground beetles and delicate cellar spiders. I am immovable like the stone on which I sit; I am part of the rock face witnessing the simple miracles that happen with each slight shift of the light. Then, a small stone is dislodged from the hillside to my right. It tumbles down, down, down and splashes into the water below, dispersing the glowing orbs only momentarily. Like a memory, it gathers itself again once the waves settle; a single luminous body of glittering light, forever putting itself together again.

I am pulled from my trance when the clouds shift and the glow dissolves. Most of the creek is now shrouded in shade. Early evening, like a light switch, has arrived. How long have I been here? The sense of time has escaped me, replaced by seemingly more powerful senses.

A fly, oblivious to the concept of stillness, finds me. Initially, I resist her, as the shift from day to evening grows and I am irritated, pleading for the light to stay a little longer. The sun has other ideas, though, and its brilliance continues to dim. The fly explores my hand. I softly wave my arm. I hope the breeze will carry her away as it seems to be carrying away my sun. No such luck. The fly is persistent in telling me to get on with it. I concede that it is time to return home. Just as I decide to make the shift and stand, the sharpness of a mosquito's bite catches me off guard. I am instantly pulled out of this sensory magic in only the way a rude mosquito can accomplish. I return to myself, to my body, and to making my way back home.

As I venture along the trail and among the trees and ferns and flowers and leaves, I am still captivated by the changing light. At each turn, the sun dips lower in the sky and the forest flares, dims and gleams, transforming with each step I take. Finally, all at once, it is subdued by dusk. Like magic, this is a new forest, different from the forest I first visited that day, and the day before, and all the days beyond, different even with each step I take though I follow the same path. When I reach the field and look out to the stone that supported me earlier that day, I see it, too, has achieved a metamorphosis.

Belonging

On one beautiful summer morning, with the sun already high in the sky and a bright day still before me, I slid on a pair of flip flops and headed to the woods. Eventually, I found myself in a once-cleared field now overgrown with sparse and spindly trees, wild roses and butterfly bushes and tangles of blackberry bushes. The flowering seasons of the rose and butterfly bushes had ended, but the blackberries were only just beginning to swell.

Pausing to take in the open space, deciding whether to follow the trail to the right or to the left and circle around to the other side of the open field, I notice that the invasive Himalayan blackberry species already has many large, deep-purple berries, whereas the native trailing blackberry, difficult to spot among the tough tangles of its rival, are still green.

The Himalayan blackberry, or *Rubus armeniacus*, originated in Armenia and northern Iran but thrives in BC's climate, so much so that it can produce up to 13,000 seeds for every square metre of growth. The dense thickets can suffocate other plant and tree species important to the local ecosystem and can act as a barrier for larger wild animals, making it impossible for them to move along their regular routes. As the story goes, American horticulturist Luther Burbank introduced the species to North America in 1885. He received a seed packet in the mail from India; believing that's where the seeds originated from, he called them the Himalayan Giant, on account that the stalk and berries were much larger than the native species. He planted them in his own backyard, and then started selling the seeds to customers throughout the Pacific Northwest in 1894.

If I look closely, I can see the difference between the two species. The trailing blackberry's vines creep along close to the ground and have tendrils with a relatively small circumference. In fact, they were given their common name "trailing" because they keep such a low profile, never overwhelming other plants nearby. Their leaves, unlike the wide and more oval-shaped broadleaf of the invasive kind, are slightly narrow and long, producing smaller flowers and then small and sweeter berries. The Himalayan blackberry, by contrast, boasts large white flowers, generally pink in the centre, with sizable berries that can be flavourless or slightly woody depending on where they grow.

Everything about the trailing blackberry—or *sqw'o:lmux̱-wulhp*, *skw'ilmuxw* or *sqw'il'muxw*, depending on whether you are up river, down river or island bound—is slightly more delicate. To me, its delicate nature demonstrates that it belongs because of the way it blends into its environment and complements other plants. It is connected to the way this forest works. On the other hand, Burbank's introduced species attempts to take over: it muscles around and over other plants; its thick and deep-rooted stalks with sharp barbs bully the forest. Of course, the trailing blackberry is resilient and refuses to be completely overtaken, but nonetheless I see the very nature of colonialism encased in every seed spreading from one place to another, every stalk that takes root, every flower that blooms and every berry produced: invasive species have a bad habit of colonizing native land. Sometimes, when I gaze into the Himalayan bush, I see myself gazing back, as if I've peered into some distorted mirror.

SUMMER OBSEQUIES

On the day that broke heat records across Canada, and some of us were hearing the phrase *heat dome* for the first time, I found myself, like everyone else, desperately attempting to escape the swelter. Transformers exploded across cities, leaving many without power and therefore no air conditioning. Those who were vulnerable and at risk of being exposed to the sun and high temperatures found relief in cooling centres or shopping malls.

We took our pets—two cats Milo and Eva and our dog, Charlie—to the basement of the main house. The cement pour set into the earth keeps the temperature low and helps to cool the remainder of the house to some extent. Throughout the heat dome, because of the 45°C weather, the basement never dropped below 20°C. I popped down to the cement floor every now and then to cool off and break away from the crushing weather.

In the barn, my dad strapped a large fan, covered with chicken wire, haphazardly to the ceiling rafters. Keeping the barn swallows, nesting with their babies, and the horses as cool as possible, was a top priority.

My preferred cooling spot on this day was in the creek.

I knew I was fortunate to have this escape. I left my shoes at home and wandered down the path, through the ferns and among the trees. The forest canopy was absorbing whatever it could of the saturating heat, as the trees swayed ever so slightly, attempting to cool the air of the understory layer with movement. Even in places where everything seemed relatively still, the breath of the forest was still there.

I was careful not to brush up against stinging nettles or disturb the ground cover too much. The air picked up a breeze and, for a brief moment, my skin felt the oppressive temperature ease. Nonetheless, even under the comparatively cooler canopy, I noted sword ferns brittle from dehydration, the wilting leaves of maple trees and stiff flower petals curling in on themselves at the edges. The plants inhale and exhale, one slow breath at a time, nearly dormant under the brutality of this weather.

As I came closer to the creek, I noted how the air cooled even more; the water was breathing with the forest, trickling and tumbling over and along the crevices of rocks and sticks, running down, down, down, cooling the environment with water from farther up the mountain. The creek achieves this despite its water level being far too low, revealing previously obscured sand and pebbles made smooth from years of running water. On this day, the bottom of the creek was exposed and I could see the ghostly remnant of the path the water had taken only a month before.

Meteorologists call it climate weirding. Usually, the earth does what it is supposed to do to keep all the working elements in check: clouds regularly release moisture and on the West Coast that means periodic rain in a relatively even amount. Temperatures rise to extremes sometimes, even sparking wildfires that, in moderation, can have some benefits for second- or third-growth forests with tall trees and little underbrush, as the fires recycle important nutrients and create the much-needed nitrogen for the ecosystem's health. Climate weirding, though, is when this natural balance is no longer functioning as it should. It rains too much, too hard, for example, and washed-out areas become vulnerable to erosion. Then, suddenly, the rain might stop. It stops for too long and then it gets too hot. The creeks begin to dry up and uncontrollable fires blaze, sometimes ignited by thunderstorms, sometimes ignited by humans. Natural forest fires and controlled burns can be necessary for the rejuvenation and rebirth of plant life in forests, but these are different from the forest fires of our climate-weirding era. Sustained heat and lack of moisture mean the bushy undergrowth burns too hot for too long. The damage is not only costing us our homes and, in the case of the residents of Lytton, BC, our cities, but it is also costing the planet a valuable source that manages the increasing levels of carbon dioxide in our atmosphere.

I approach the creek and dip my toes into a small trickle of cool water. I begin to walk upstream, avoiding the still-slippery stones where moss and slimy membranes have built up over the seasons. I feel the breath of the forest, but it feels more like a pant. I am followed by hungry mosquitos and other winged critters also enjoying the coolness of the creek but too preoccupied with the need to rest to bother with me. Two ravens chime in, either announcing my presence to one another, asking me to leave or not noticing me at all and rather sharing with the forest some knowledge reserved for these forest inhabitants. To my left is a small trail weaving among wilting huckleberry and wild blueberry bushes yet to produce their fruit, too narrow for a human. It must be how deer, young black bears or porcupines creep up and down the rocky sides of the water source looking for a drink. To my right is a jagged rock wall adorned with varieties of moss and lichen; maidenhead ferns grow out of the many smaller gaps that stagger the larger caverns, the homes of frogs, spiders and salamanders lucky enough to have prime real estate at this time of year, right on the water's edge. The air is notably cooler in front of this rock edifice.

Continuing upstream, I finally find a pool deep enough to submerge myself into—barely. It's carved out at the base of the rock wall; maidenhead ferns jut and trace ripples on the surface of the creek. The water is cool and dark and the rocks, not quite submerged but still damp, have a certain glisten to them. The only sounds I hear are the gibbering ravens and slow and delicate but continuous *plop-plop-dribble-plop-plop* from the trickle of water cascading down the rock wall. When this waterfall rages in the spring, winter or fall, it is deafeningly loud—too loud sometimes to even hear my own thoughts. I must stand much farther back on the creek bank, as the water crashes hard into itself and the large stone-filled pools below. I certainly wouldn't be able to sit at the base of it. On that day, I find it hard to believe the amount of water that typically descends here.

One limb at a time, I slowly sink into the water and lean

back into its cool embrace. The relief is astounding. I duck my head under and grab hold of a large rock at the centre of the creek; for a moment, I stay suspended like that, letting my feet and legs float downstream, feeling my hair cascade around my shoulders, listening to the muffled sounds of underwater life. I lift my head back up and climb up onto the stone, settling myself in a cross-legged position. I am finally cool. The unforgiving sun is peeking between the tops of the trees, but with my wet eyelashes, everywhere I look seems to shimmer.

I am completely alone—except that I am not really alone. Sitting next to me, perched on a ledge that juts out from the rock face, is a small brown frog. It is as if that ledge were made for him. The entire time I am there, he never moves. Hovering above me, drinking from the water trickling down the rock face of the now dribbling waterfall, is a pair of green hummingbirds. In a skinny cedar tree five feet away, its branches stretching out over the creek, are two robin nestlings whose mother flies out from her perch to find food and drink, then returns to the silent open mouths of her babies. I'm concerned about their silence, remembering the racket of the barn swallows in the spring. They should be making more noise than they are.

I do my best to blend in. I breathe the space in and back out. After some time relaxing this way, I notice that the mother robin has not returned. I watch for her. I wait for her. The nestlings' beaks hang over the edge of the twig-crafted home, agape and waiting. Their heads remain still, beaks open. For a moment I fear the worst: the heat has killed them. Then, one head adjusts ever so slightly to signal life. Then another and another. They are alive.

But not every animal on Sumas Mountain, let alone the wider Fraser Valley, coastline and interior, has access to a fresh creek during the heat dome to stay cool. I feel the panic in my chest rise as I think of the farm animals under those tin roofs in the valley, the marine life in the too-warm pools left on the rocky beaches after the tide rolls out, the wildlife in drier areas. The relief I have felt in this creek begins to feel absurd, other-worldly, not right. Then, suddenly, a rock comes crashing down the edifice, breaking my train of thought. I look to try and spot the source of the rock but instead spot the mother bird. She sits some distance from her babies, and from me. She is not approaching her nest and not retreating but rather hopping side to side on a branch several feet from the nest, her head pointed in my direction.

I suddenly realize that I may be the reason she has not returned. Having spotted me at some point, she has likely deemed me as a threat. I wait a short moment to see if she will come back to feed her babies, but as she continues to hop impatiently and the nestlings grow more still, I know that if I am there, she might not come back. She is stressed. The forest is stressed. My presence is not helping and I decide that my time at the creek has come to an end for the day.

I take my leave, allowing the forest to resume its rhythm. I do not belong here, not really. Gratitude, though, seizes me as I take one step farther away from that one cool and restful place. I will retreat to the cement palace of my basement.

Pacing the parched brown lawn, I edge barefoot along white fences and fence posts, pausing at every dehydrated plant— reeds without water, nettle that lost its sting, shrivelled pink foxgloves and dried-up mushrooms. I feel their thirst and look to the sky to beckon for rain. I call out but make no sound. My eyes widen and my arms reach out. I urge the cloudless skies to gather moisture and release it. I wait in yearning until a single drop falls on my cheek. Then another, and another. I look down to the ground and the grass changes before my eyes as rain falls all around me—drops full and fat with entire worlds contained within their clear, glistening orbs. I feel absolute relief. The plants beckon me to them and we dance together bathed in rainfall.

I am awoken by the sound of an abstract tinkling. It takes me a moment to orient myself to wakeful life. The soft light in my loft tells me it is the beginning of dawn. Was that mystical sound the long-awaited raindrops on my tin roof? Was it real? Did it finally come? Suddenly energized, I slide out of bed and lean up against the open windows. Rain. My mind and body come alive as the dewy scent of moisture greets me. I take in every molecule of freshness.

Making my way to the door, I skipped over a pair of hard-bottomed slippers, threw on a light-grey bathrobe and, giddy to feel the wet earth beneath my feet, slipped silently out the door—barefoot. I padded down the steps and toed gingerly through a gravel threshold until I landed at last on the wet earth. I stood in the light but steady precipitation and watched as every drop kissed the ground, a well-remembered and dearly missed encounter between earth and sky. There was a thickness to the air only possible during moments such as this—when life breathes a great sigh of relief after a long wait.

Wetness creeped along the base of my feet and along the crevices of my toes as I remained standing in the grass. Head uncovered, feet bare; water fell all around me, through me. The forest bordering our property shimmered in the clouded, fading starlight of dawn; the earth stretched up to match my curved soles. I listened as I heard first one, then another, and then many birds wake to find their forest home changed. Soon, I was bathed not only in that refreshing rain but also in the beautiful, deafening cacophony of morning birds.

Watching the land and forest drink in this nectar from above, I spotted, tucked in the trees nearby, a swallow. Perched beneath a large maple leaf, she looked relatively dry as she regarded the tumbling water. We stood together, the swallow and I, listening, witnessing, waiting—for what I wasn't sure.

Lost in the thrum, I reached out my hand to catch and hold what moisture I could. Then, with the slight movement of a breeze, slim yellow rays reached across the landscape from where the rain had just stopped falling. Just like that, the sun began to rise and the rainfall that broke the heat ended. The swallow chirps, calling for her mate, who returns the note from somewhere behind me. She takes off to meet her partner and I watch as they soar throughout the air together. They had each sought refuge from the falling water in a separate place.

I am led by the rich fragrance of damp foliage into the wilderness. That heavy scent felt like a clear sign of the forests' rejuvenation. The forest is enchanted.

Still barefoot and in my light bathrobe, I walk deeper into the thickness of the trees and, as I do, the air becomes heavier. An even greater abundance of weighted scents emerges. I waltz slowly along narrow paths, loving the droplets of water brushing off sword ferns and onto my calves and knees. My hands graze the tallest ground cover and gently move aside branches heavy with rain that are now slightly bent or leaning. The masses of spider webs that were strung up across the trail are now few; only the strongest, largest and better-placed webs remain. They glisten as the clouds continue to part and the sun continues to rise; slivers of the cool light of dawn illuminate droplets sitting on silk strings like weightless diamonds.

Each part of this forest has various neighbourhoods of trees where certain species thrive, gather together and create their own micro-ecosystem. At the southern end of the trail, a new thick scent emerges. The syrupy sweetness of vine maples hits me first, then a heavy warmth of black walnuts. I continue along, breathing wet heat from heavily baked and recently soaked pine needles and fallen maple leaves. As I enter a thicket of western red cedar, it's impossible not to taste the sharp flavour of the bark permeating the air. I walk slowly among these smells and sights for I don't know how long, getting lost in thought as I drift, rejuvenated, from place to place, my feet soaking up whatever moisture has permeated the earth—I carry it with me all the way home.

Meeting Hades

When the heat dome finally subsided by mid-July 2021, I learned about the damage this event produced—an event that, according to researchers at the University of Washington, could not have happened without human-caused climate change. A total of 619 people in BC died due to excessive heat and dehydration—most of these people were elderly, children or homeless. An estimated 660,000 farm animals overheated and suffocated. Up and down BC's southern coast, there were approximately one billion marine wildlife deaths. When I visited Kitsilano Beach in Vancouver shortly after the heat dome, I could smell death before I could see it: the rot of marine life. It is uncertain at the time of writing this book how far the implications of this heat dome may reach, and there are many scientists who claim it is foolish to believe that this will be our last one.

By mid-July, mask mandates for pandemic-related reasons had eased, but around this time, BC's Ministry of Health recommended that masks should be worn outdoors because of the distressing air quality from the forest fires. I had watched as the sky that summer—the heat dome summer, the COVID-19 summer—went from clear and blue to grey and dull and, eventually, yellow, red and pale brown. The sickly coloured air closed in around us, coming from the east and the west, slithering through forests and across open waters, until everything was saturated with wildfire smoke. Reaching out and touching the railing of a deck or a car parked outside or a maple leaf left my hand with a layer of soot. Rubbing my fingers together, feeling the grittiness between them, and looking out into an unfamiliar sky, I felt sure I knew of dystopia.

Breathing became an issue for the young, the elderly and those with compromised lungs. We were encouraged to remain indoors and, if we had to go outside, wear a mask. This was difficult, to say the least: we'd been quarantining, isolating and social distancing in our homes for so long that the thought of doing it all again—in what should be the most marvellous time of year—was a challenge for many of us. It was devastating to be kept from the natural beauty by a wall of impermeable yellow smoke.

One day, I decided to take my car into town just to get out of the house. I walked the several feet from my loft to my parked car and could taste the sour air. My hair was ashen and dull by the time I was in the driver's seat. I soon found out that driving through wildfire smoke was akin to the sightlessness one experiences when driving through a snowstorm. I made it several blocks down the road before I decided to turn around: I couldn't see the edge of the road, how far in the distance a stop sign was or whether someone or something was in my path. It was dangerous. So, I returned home and from there watched the world around me disappear. When I looked out the window, I felt trapped by an environment my species had created.

But there was more. In June 2021, researchers discovered 751 unmarked graves of Indigenous children near the former Marieval Indian Residential School in Saskatchewan. This came just after Tk'emlúps te Secwépemc First Nation used ground-penetrating radar to discover 215 child remains on the grounds of the former Kamloops Indian Residential School. Further evidence of the undocumented deaths of Indigenous children while at residential schools continued to be searched for and revealed across the country.

What world, what reality, what hell were we living in? A sickening ache burrowed into the deepest parts of my stomach. I was teaching students in Abbotsford when I first learned of those numbers—215, 751. How is it possible that any school could have a graveyard?

In those first moments, I failed to presume any adequate or clear language to talk about this discovery. A *discovery*. Is that the right word? How does one *discover* evidence of what so many had participated in and actively concealed? Uncover. Maybe that's the word. Maybe there is no word suited to match what we see when we peel back the carefully laid veil of history.

If the heat dome, wildfires and pandemic felt dystopian, the uncovering of child graves across the country is something else entirely. An unreality.

As I choked on the smoke created by a world that ploughs over environments in the name of growth, those graves were there, are still there, amidst it all. We were suffocating in the heat, feeling trapped in the sightlessness of thick toxic air, and muscling our way through a global pandemic, but we were, at the very least, alive to feel it. There is a responsibility in this truth—to sit in the smouldering unreality of our time and *feel* it. Feel the difficulty and the strangle of oppression. Struggle to breathe, to find the words that fit the disillusioned pit at the core of us, then learn what can be done about it.

What's in a Name?

Sunday, August 8, 2021. The morning sun anchored itself low in the sky, filtering through maples, birch, cedars and firs, casting dusty-gold and yellow hues across our property. I packed my car with a hammock, water, food, boots, extra socks and some homemade bug spray, slammed the trunk door closed and then slid into the front seat. As I drove by the young pin oak my father planted at the end of our driveway the year before, I caught a slight translucent glimmer through the small green and pointy-ended leaves that burst from every branch. The rubbery, wet-looking surface of the young leaves gave the illusion that there had been recent moisture— but there hadn't been adequate moisture in months. The heat dome had thankfully ended, but the province was scarred. We were all scarred and tired and scared. The need for quiet had settled within me. Those beautiful young pin oak leaves mocked me.

I was headed to Lund, not knowing what to look for or what I hoped to find. Lund—the most northern town along BC's Sunshine Coast, mile zero at the end of Highway 101, a seaside village one hundred and twenty kilometres north of Vancouver. It is known by some as the shellfish capital, by others as the gateway to Desolation Sound. Visited in 1792 by Captain George Vancouver, Lund (or Klah ah men) had a long history before it's so-called *discovery*. The Tla'amin, Klahoose and Homalco First Nations have lived in, fished and loved this part of coastal BC, sharing forests and ocean shores, abundant with thriving ocean species, berries and deer, since time immemorial.

When Lund was settled by Charles Thulin, the Salish were nearly decimated by the smallpox epidemic that swept through communities across Canada at the time of Western colonization. This aided the ease of Western European settlement. Captain Vancouver criticized Lund and Desolation Sound for its "awful silence" and "gloomy forests," a hard sell to anyone who visits the area today.

It is this silence I am drawn to, what I aim to be lost in. To disconnect from the noise of modern life and the madness of a world teetering on an edge, the centre crumbling—this is why I go to the woods. I chase a connection, one I may never fully achieve, though I seek it still. Although I was born in BC, though the coast and the mountains, trees, waterways, birds and the rains and the air are all in my heart and blood, in every choice I make, I am a product of colonizers. My connection with this land is tainted by the haunted past of land usurpers. So, I go to the woods to learn, to see and to connect in the best way I know how.

My journey to Lund begins with the crunching gravel of my driveway on Sumas Mountain. I turn right onto the blackened-asphalt street and watch the pin oak and her leaves fade from view in the rear-view mirror. Left on Dawson Road.

Left again on Sumas Mountain Road. I follow this road downward, passing the tremendous Kinder Morgan oil storage towers glinting white above the tree canopy. At the bottom of the mountain, I head toward what was once Sumas Lake and merge onto Highway 1, the main artery linking cities east and west of Abbotsford, a network of roads to houses and farms, and land occupied by cattle and chickens, blueberries and raspberries, and one field of u-pick tulips in the spring. This is the result of what city planners in 1920 called "land reclamation": land which had been "found" beneath Sumas Lake was *claimed* and given to white settler farmers, many of whose farms are still in the hands of their descendants one hundred years later.

The Big Drain began in 1920. It took nearly four years to finish the water evacuation after the Barrowtown pump station and the Sumas Canal were completed. During this time, new farm owners were pulling dozens of sturgeon—fish descendants from the early Jurassic epoch—out of the drying lake bed every day. I drive over this "reclaimed" area today, long after the lake has been emptied, as I head west toward Langley, Surrey, Coquitlam and Vancouver.

From Abbotsford, the colossal highway system is a bottleneck of exhaust and individualism. Everyone needs their own car. Everyone has somewhere to go. Including me.

Along the fluctuating parking lot of bumper-to-bumper traffic I go. There is something about the strip of highway between Abbotsford and Langley that feels particularly competitive. Dump trucks groan heavily with their beds full of gravel, loaded semis shudder; we all gear down, gear up, attempt to find our pace. Teslas tailgate, a yellow GMC Hummer bullies its way forward to close the gap between it and the turbo diesel Volkswagen in front, tail lights glowing red as its brake is engaged. Stress does not touch me in this white-knuckle stretch of roadway; thankfully, I left the mountain with extra hours to spare before my 10:00 a.m. sailing to Langdale from the Horseshoe Bay ferry terminal in West Vancouver. I simply drive with the flow, slowing and resuming speed with the herd.

I inch slowly over the Port Mann bridge, pass the Ikea warehouse and Burnaby Lake, not visible from the road, as well as a casino and hotels and billboards reminding parents to talk to their kids about heroin and that McDonald's burgers are "crafted for your craving." Crossing the Ironworkers Memorial Bridge, traffic begins to thin slightly. Highway 1 turns into the Sea-to-Sky or Highway 99.

Climbing, climbing, climbing. The road becomes narrow and cuts through mountainous terrain lined with coniferous Douglas fir, western red cedar, western hemlock, grand fir, Sitka spruce and western yew, each a unique shade of green that is woven into the forest array. The highway overlooks the Burrard Inlet, the city vanishing and Vancouver Island misty in the distance, a breathtaking view that continues farther north toward settler-stolen land that was once sectioned into mining and logging towns and has now become the trendy neighbourhoods and resorts of Britannia Beach, Squamish and Whistler. My route, however, culminates at the Horseshoe Bay terminal; I take the right-hand exit to Keith Road and end up in a long line-up of cars, trucks, campers, vans and motorcyclists packed tight with family, gear, toys, snacks and pets, for whatever journey awaits on the other side of the water.

With the better part of an hour until sailing, I roll down my car window and listen to the sounds of Cypress Mountain. I watch wind and sun skirt among the crowd of cars, whispering at this obtuse expression of modernity before returning to the backdrop of land and water—wondering, I imagine, why nobody listens. I see Wind go into the trees, over the mountain and out to sea, leaving in its wake an eerie breeze-free warmth that settles in around us. A remnant of the heat dome.

Despite the many signs and announcements demanding otherwise, a few vehicle engines remain running as we wait for the boarding call. The ferry line grows. A Toyota 4Runner idles with a steady whirring moan. A green Subaru Outback has a loping purr. The Dodge Ram's bull snort contrasts with the theremin-like whirring of the Chevrolet Bolt EV. Their engines remain running, I assume, so their passengers can sit in the air conditioning. I check the thermostat: it's 26°C and not even ten o'clock. We remain there, locked in our parking space, until the ferry arrives and the announcement comes from the loudspeaker asking everyone to prepare to load. The individual vehicle voices drown out as the cascade of engines erupt, impatient to take their place on the ferry.

Once loaded, lane by lane, car by car, packing as many as possible into the multi-levelled ferry boat, followed by foot passengers arriving via the gangway linking land and vessel, the ship roars to life. Drivers and passengers leave their vehicles and make their way up to the main deck. A few remain in their cars, reading books, taking naps, snacking on sandwiches and banana bread brought from home. Some pets are left napping with a window cracked. I follow the crowd, making my way up steel steps, passing the gift shop, help-yourself café and White Spot restaurant. I walk by passengers who have found a seat next to the large windows to cozy up against throughout the sailing. I pull on a heavy iron door, painted white, that takes me out to the deck.

The *Queen of Coquitlam* horn blasts as it leaves port, heading northwest to the Sunshine Coast peninsula. It slowly chugs through Howe Sound, skirting between Bowen and Keats islands to the left, Gambier and Anvil islands to the right; farther south, through the Burrard Inlet and across the Strait of Georgia, are Gabriola and Vancouver islands. As the ferry picks up speed, my ears become full of the cacophonous rush of moving water and ocean air. On this summer morning the crossing is beautiful, and not just because of the view, but also because I feel as though I can witness every passenger, once loaded and settled, exhale the weight of the world for a moment. On deck, they wander from front to back and side to side, serenely looking out at the water, long hair whipping in the wind. We all watch as the ship cuts through the ocean surface like glass. They chat, read books and sit and listen to the sounds of the ocean, the sounds of the ferry itself, dozing as they lean against the steely white beast carrying them across the water.

I settle myself into a corner within the port-side exterior wall to hide from the powerful wind and increasingly brighter

sun. From this vantage point, I notice a couple sitting in the
sun against the outer railing, their golden retriever loung-
ing at their feet. The retriever's ears perk up each time one
of them takes a bite of their shared burrito. Once or twice,
they concede to the pleas of their pet. Next to them, I see the
name of the ferry spelled out across a handrail. The *Queen
of Coquitlam*. Coquitlam. An anglicization of kʷikʷəƛ̓əm, or
Kwikwetlem Nation. *Queen of* Coquitlam. The preposition
of can suggest ownership: the Queen's Coquitlam. This is a
power move that signifies colonialism and the reach of impe-
rial power in Canada.

How else do I participate in these "power moves" made
long ago through the act of naming? *Sumas* is a Halqemeylem
word meaning "big level opening," but the Sumas First Nation calls the mountain Kw'ekw'e'iːqw, pronounced *Kw-ewk-
weeuwkw*. The valley in which it is located, Fraser Valley, is
named after the Scottish explorer and fur trader Simon Fraser
who built the first European settlement in British Columbia.
British Columbia—the name Queen Victoria gave the area
when it became an official colony in 1858, instead of New
Caledonia, the name Fraser suggested. I am on the *Queen of
Coquitlam* and the ferry is on the Howe Sound, Alt'ka7tsem.
Once the ferry docks, I will be travelling through Gibsons,
the unceded land of the Sḵwx̱wú7mesh Úxwumixw, which
we call in English the Squamish First Nation. The district
of Sechelt recently changed the name of Saltery Bay back to
skelhp, the name used by the shíshálh Nation, traditional
caretakers of the land. I like the way the accents and numbers and punctuation resist easy pronunciation from my

English-speaking tongue. Naming has a power over the way we view and understand the land and waters we are a part of. I have a responsibility to understand this. A simple name can erase so much in a single utterance.

Once the ferry lands in Langdale, I catch the Sunshine Coast Highway directly out of the terminal and head toward sk̲elh (Earls Cove), twenty-seven kilometres north. Passing through shíshálh (Sechelt), xwilkway (Halfmoon Bay) and salalus (Madeira Park), the island road is largely bordered by tall, lean evergreens, with the occasional glimpse of the ocean rushing in to kiss the land.

Just under an hour and a half later, I arrive at Earls Cove. This ferry (recently renamed from *Island Sky* to *Malaspina Sky* after Alessandro Malaspina, a noble-birthed Italian in the Spanish navy and explorer of these coasts—not exactly a move toward reconciliation) is much smaller than the *Queen of Coquitlam*. The operations are modest and less hectic, and most vehicles turn their engines off as they wait despite the heat. The sounds of the forest take over—the rustling of the wind in the trees, chittering squirrels chasing one another up tall, straight cedars, the call of seafaring gulls and the screeching, chirping, cry of an osprey nearby. Although the boat arrives and departs on time, everything seems to run in true coastal form: everyone who wears BC Ferries jackets, as well as the passengers, are calm and relaxed. They doze here and there, settling into a slower way of life. The destination, I realize, isn't the point. Instead, the point is the path that's bringing me to wherever it is that I'm going—this path that demands a slowness, which in turn allows me to hear the call to bear witnesses to this place as it is on this day in this moment in time. I don't know what or who exactly is calling me, but I can hear it. The *way there*—to the end, to the goal, to paradise—is the story to tell.

Feeling suddenly grateful for my little vacation, I begin to wax poetic about the ferry as a concept. *Ferries*, I think in my reverie, *are like Zen Buddhist teachers*. They demand that we slow down and encourage our contemplation, which can help release the tension humanity loves to create.

Parked and comfortable, I watch the cars line up behind me. They park one after another, many with blue and green kayaks strapped to their roofs. Raspberry-red coolers with popcorn-white lids are packed into trunks alongside lemon-yellow duffel bags, canvas grocery bags, dogs and kids devouring Subway sandwiches and bags of Lays potato chips. Some I recognize from my first ferry crossing earlier that day. They too are venturing farther up the coast. They too are being directed by the cheery, relaxed traffic director. They too are silenced by the quiet of this place. They too, I'm sure, are eager to dive into the green woods, to connect, to see, to experience and seek an understanding of what it means to be human in a natural space.

After landing in skelhp, I meet up with another section of the Sunshine Coast Highway—another gorgeous stretch that weaves in and around cozy seaside villages and marinas where water laps against the hulls of small and tall boats owned by families and fishermen. Once I leave behind the crowd of cars from the ferry, traffic is light and slow allowing space to look out to the Strait of Georgia. I watch sunlight glisten on the water's surface as it gently laps the shorelines of beaches dotted with people walking and enjoying the view. Opposite the water side of this road there is forest: tall, narrow island trees cover much of this place in deep green splendour—the most beautiful West Coast paradise that a road can reach.

In Powell River, I pick up palak paneer on rice from Royal Zayka and I am delighted to find it is some of the most sensational Indian food I've eaten in some time. Afterward, I drive farther down the highway; just before the Shinglemill Pub, I turn into a small nook off the highway right before the trailhead that will take me from Shinglemill to Mowat Bay. I have a few minutes to gather my gear before L. arrives.

I discovered L. on an online community forum; she helps hikers get to and from trailheads that are difficult to navigate, she comes to their rescue if something goes wrong and she offers great advice on anything related to the Sunshine Coast. That night, I will sleep in my backcountry hammock in L.'s backyard; the next morning, I will wander the six kilometres to Klah ah men, where my walking journey really begins. The multi-day hut-to-hut adventure will take me along the coast and into the mountains; there, I will walk among emerald-green lakes and frothing waterfalls, old-growth tree groves, trickling creeks and sweeping views of the Salish Sea. The paths have been well maintained since their initial build in the early 1990s; the entire system is one hundred and eighty kilometres, separated into manageable sections by huts built by local volunteers that you can camp or rest in. My trip will take me from Sarah Point back to my car at the Shinglemill Pub: a total of fifty-two kilometres, departing from the ocean and weaving through dense forests and up rocky mountainsides, I planned to complete in three days. The rest of the trail would have to wait for another time.

While I wait for L., I breathe in the coastal atmosphere of Powell River. It is on a peninsula and not an island, despite only being accessible by ferry, although it feels like a small island town. It is isolated from the world by ocean, inlets and mountains, and it is this separateness from larger and more populated locations on the West Coast that makes it attractive. I am lulled by the enormity of the trees and the savoury ocean scent wafting in from the inlet nearby as vehicles periodically whir past and smiling hikers, some with dogs, some with kids, come and go from the trailhead, their boots crunching the gravel. They smile at me with soft eyes, as if they know some secret to life. Nobody says anything to me as they prepare to enter the chapel of trees, but their nonverbal greetings are warm, welcoming and intoxicating, like the arms of the trees themselves, beckoning me to move among them. It is easy to drink up the aura of this area, to fold into the background of Place. But if I let myself, I can transcend where I am in the present moment and shift into wondering what was erased and rewritten.

L. arrives, meeting me where I have parked. Platinum blonde with a popsicle-orange T-shirt, she greets me and loads my gear into the back of her Dodge. She is a talker. She wants me to know how many times she has walked the trail. Six. She tells me there is very little water out there in the creeks and streams, on account of the heat dome. She reminds me that smoke from the wildfires on the eastern edge of BC may impact the air as I start my walk. She affirms that starting the trip from a water taxi at Sarah Point, via Lund, is the best way to begin. She warns about bears and the need to hang my food in a tree far enough away from camp each night. She makes me promise that I will call her if I get stuck someplace, roll an ankle or just can't go any farther. She wants me to know that this trail, this place, is heaven on earth. I listen, drinking every word in. My excitement builds as we drive down the highway, farther from Powell River and closer to her home.

L.'s property is heavily treed with firs. They line the long dirt driveway leading away from the road, winding through her five-acre piece of land and ending at the back of the property. There, in a small clearing, having left the remainder of the land untouched, is a newly built modest home with a modern design. Aiming for a smaller footprint, the house is a standing rectangle with three stories and a skillion roof. Each floor has large, black-framed windows, strong focal points that contrast with the burnt-orange standing seam metal siding, grey concrete patio and darkly stained wood cover. Immediately surrounding the house are stones of various sizes, levelled and layered with native plants—sword fern, maidenhair fern, deer fern, thimbleberries, Oregon grape and madrones. There is no lawn; L. has left the landscaping to nature. L. has named this place tagəkəayən, the Tla'amin word for *fern*. Staying here is the perfect end to a road of contemplation, setting the tone to start my walk.

The evening passes slowly. Peacefully. As the sun begins

to dip, squirrels race amok from tree to tree, hoarding their spoils. I lay in my hammock, rain cover off, mosquito net zipped tight, and quietly watch the stars and moon and deep blue of the night sky glide through time. I hear mosquitos hum and owls hoot. Something yips and howls somewhere in the distance. This night parade of sonorous sounds reminds me of Sumas—of the wilderness it once was.

When I sit still during some summer evenings on Sumas, I can hear the echoes of that wilderness of the past. It floats in on the air of a crisp night when the rest of the world is quiet and unmoving. I hear the mosquitoes humming, the owls hooting, the coyotes yipping, and there is no distraction. I become suspended in a time where progress has yet to interfere with the secrets of the forest at night. In L.'s backyard, I drift off to sleep in my hammock and dream of Sumas Mountain, but in my dream it has no name.

Only Connect

One of the youngest residents living on our Charlie Spruce Place property is often found wandering the fields and amongst the trees with his mother. Little two-year-old feet stepping through the tall and small grasses. He lives with his family in the rental suite. In the summer, his naked toes fold in and around the smallest variations of the earth. As a toddler, wobbly and teetering everywhere he goes, this child checks out *everything* in his backyard. His short but quick gait directs him to actively seek out new artefacts for discovery, ready to examine through sight, sound, touch, smell and taste—yes, to his mother's chagrin, taste too. At times, he babbles at a rock or blade of grass or strange bug, reaching out and feeling it, asking questions in his own little language.

His mother, who follows him closely, encourages him to be curious, to play and to learn what this place is all about. She allows him to lead the way, offering assurance when he's uncertain and telling him stories about everything she knows about whatever strange object he happens upon in his adventures. From my window, I can see the two of them traipsing about. He stops to look at something lodged in the dirt and points a pudgy-baby arm in the mystery item's direction, then another arm and index finger at the same object, impatiently directing his mother to what he has discovered. She, ever aware of where he is, slowly meanders over, not in any hurry. She is patient and gentle, allowing him to explore on his own.

Meeting her son, she bends down and hovers on the balls of her feet, bare like his, and asks what he has found. The child points to the object and she begins a narrative. His gaze grows more intense as his face comes nearer and nearer the earth, then bends his ear downward as if attempting to listen to what it has to say for itself. His mother grows silent, watching and waiting. Then, as if satisfied with her explanations and the silent response from the earthly element, he raises his head, chin proud at learning this new secret of the universe, and toddles off toward a neighbouring item quite close by. He looks at the item, points to it with those swollen baby hands, looks inquisitively at his mother and waits for her input and for more of the tales that each thing he finds may have to offer.

Not long after this ritual of wandering, seeing, questioning and listening begins, mother and son are joined by two cats and our dog, Charlie. The five of them, like a band of rather slow yet hopeful cartoon adventurers, spend some more time moving about the property, slowly winding from spot to spot, at the edge of the forest, in the forest, through the fields, along creeks and atop fallen trees. There is no agenda, no plan, no place to be or rush off to. There is only the desire to learn and explore.

Like the child, the animals move around in tow. They smell and watch, engaging in a curious dialogue between nature and the self. Perhaps wild things out in the world engage in similar practices. Aristotle once exclaimed that plants and animals have souls, or psyches. I wonder if this tiny human feels that existence.

One summer afternoon, my niece, sitting on the steps behind my house and looking into the trees and forest beyond, spoke to me about the way she sees the world in such a matter-of-fact way it was hard not to follow her six-year-old logic.

"Do you hear that?" my niece asked me in the heat of the day, her head tilted to one side and her large blue eyes scanning the woods we had come out of after a short afternoon walk.

"What?" I replied, trying to follow her gaze and pinpoint what she had heard.

"That," she cocked her head to the opposite side.

"The cars?" I asked, hearing a series of vehicles revving their engines as they climbed the hill along the road beyond our forest.

"No," she shook her head and continued to listen to something elusive to me.

"The gravel mine?" I prodded, my attention pulled from the cars to the distant rumbling and grinding of the mine in the opposite direction.

"No," my niece smiled patiently, her gaze boring farther into the forest.

"Me talking?" I nudged her with my elbow and quietly laughed.

"No," she giggled.

"What do you hear?" I had not the slightest clue where her attention was focussed.

"The trees, Auntie. I hear the trees."

I turned my head in a tilt like hers and looked deeply into the woods. It was then that I noticed the wind that had gently and quietly picked up. It was rustling the trees; their leaves and branches shivered, bumping against each other. The maples glistened and shuddered, their broad leaves grazing the surfaces of one another and creating a nearly inaudible sound to those conditioned into a constantly distracted state by modern human activity, by their adult humanness. The cedars and firs, bigger and slower in their movements like ancient uncles, creaked as the weight of their evergreen branches swayed, full bodied but gentle. When the wind blew harder, the trees shuddered more, each emitting their own pitch and tone—an entire orchestra working together.

Every instrument in this band was unique in its reaction to the slightest force of air. One could listen closely, just as my niece was doing, and pinpoint the different sounds and where they came from: rustle from the left, creak from the right, swish and groan dead ahead and everywhere a tinkling like rainfall coming from the rounded shape of alder leaves. The mountain was alive with movement and music. My young niece heard it.

"They are whispering to each other," she said. "Now they are singing," she added when a gust arose, urging the forest and both of us into a moment of exaltation.

FALL

Who robbed the woods,

The trusting woods?

The unsuspecting trees

Brought out their burrs and mosses

His fantasy to please.

He scanned their trinkets, curious,

He grasped, he bore away.

What will the solemn hemlock,

What will the fir-tree say?

— "Who Robbed the Woods," Emily Dickinson (1859)

BUMBLEBEES
AND ROADKILL

Fall arrives on Sumas Mountain when the light in the trees turns soft. The summer's unforgiving sun mercifully dims ever so slightly and filters through the leaves' changing colours as they morph from many shades of green to earthy oranges, reds and browns. In years not marked by various environmental disasters, trees will slowly evolve their form, moving from full and lively to dormant and sparse in colourfully changing fashion. The fall following the heat dome summer did not see lively foliage; many leaves did not change to their typical yellow, orange or red, but instead faded to brown before falling to the earth. By October, I noticed many confused trees holding onto their dead leaves long after they should have begun discarding them. Did those trees get any opportunity to prepare for a harsh winter? And yet, whether the forests are prepared or not, fall approaches.

The summer doesn't turn to autumn at a single point in time, when the evening clock's minute hand ticks from 9:03 to 9:04, marking that eternal moment when daylight and darkness perfectly align for the fall equinox. Most years, autumn is a thousand colourful vignettes filled with harsh beauties that are all too easy to pass by. On Sumas Mountain, the transition is a fast one. I have been guilty of failing to notice the changing foliage, too busy to breathe in that sweet, musty heaviness that lingers on the wind as decaying leaves collect in hidden corners, blow across streets, lawns and parks. I have never seen the first leaf fall.

But I have seen other maple leaves detach and flutter to the earth, carried down by invisible silk. I have seen the sun set over the westward wall of trees, igniting the sky in a colourful crescendo of diffused light. And I have heard the deafening crunch and shuffle as my boots lead me through knee-high piles of dried birch and walnut foliage. Walnuts and other shells stack up in barn attics and woodsheds as critters prepare for the winter; beetles scurry across paths rushing to wherever beetles go.

Often, at the onset of October, the sun shines in the part of the Fraser Valley where Sumas Lake once was, just north of the United States border. Yet if one was to look up to the mountain called Sumas, there, the fog and weather hugs the highland. It encloses the peaks and forests in voluptuous mist. Sumas Mountain exists in its own microclimate. After the hot, dry summer, it joyfully weeps with rain as creeks and streams begin to swell; the plants and trees have water again. This is the beginning of autumn on Sumas Mountain.

One fall afternoon, as I was wandering among the trees and leaves and earth, I noted how I was breathing in the sighs of the forest—relief after recent rainfall. It had been a hellish summer. The last of the heat had clung tightly to early fall days until it gave way to West Coast rains. My skin felt the forest exhaling and inhaling, helping itself and all the myriad of plant and critter species prepare for the cold. Refreshed, I wandered slowly. Deliberately. I drank every molecule of the woods that I could. When I arrived home, I found a seat on my back porch, faced the woods from which I came and watched it go about its afternoon.

Hidden in the corner of a silky, silver web, she laid in wait. It had been days, maybe weeks, since her last meal, and the recent winds had torn the geometrically perfect trap and created a dime-sized hole near the top left corner, from which a nearly invisible line attaches itself to a strong base. All four corners are holding, but the centre remains the strongest. When the sun shines in just the right way, her web is invisible. Only someone with a keen eye will see the spider sitting patiently among the flowers. She is beautiful.

Bees and flies and wasps and butterflies flit about here and there, gathering pollen. They don't notice the glistening web or its maker. They are busy; they have a job to do and they attend to it. Butterflies—blue, white, yellow—are the most non-committal as they flutter from this flower to the next, then to a tree branch, and then they float away, dancing with one another, up, up, up. Flies and wasps are less abundant but still gather for the feast.

By far the most dedicated to the task at hand are the bees. Their bee bums, held up by wings defying physics, stick out of flower cups as they fill their pant legs with the yellow stuff. They don't stay long in one spot before backing out and taking off to the next flower. Wild and farmed mason bees, honeybees, bumblebees and carpenter bees are everywhere. Upon closer inspection, I see how each species has its own unique look: some are fat and fluffy while others are trim and sleek. Colour patterns vary between the childhood memory of the yellow- and white-striped variety to nearly all black.

The feast goes on and on as the bees work alongside one another, in tandem with flies and butterflies and wasps and the occasional observing dragonfly. All the while, that spider is watching. In a split second, a single bee, laser focussed on getting to the next best pot of pollen, lands dead centre in the near-invisible trap. Instantly, the spider is there. She has hustled from her hiding place and is spinning silk. Turning and turning and turning, the bee frantically buzzes. He vibrates and thrashes, trying to tear himself free from the sticky cocoon growing thicker around him. The spider does nothing but spin. The noise from the bee increases as panic sets in. The bee is losing. With movement completely restricted by a tight silk cocoon, the bee grows quieter and more still until it becomes silent.

In a matter of seconds, the stoic spider has captured a bee much bigger than her. The spider shifts focus and moves about her web, reaching her long legs out to fix any damage before returning to her prize and moving it to one corner. She will eat well for a time.

My deck, running along the eastern edge of the property line with long boughs of cedars within arm's reach, is private for me yet welcoming to all manner of insects. Beyond it lay the secret happenings of Sumas Mountain, where critters roam, soar and scatter, and where vine maples and cedars and the remnants of ancient trees spread their roots in support of the diverse ecosystem that exists there. I love to wander among the trails, smelling each season of the year, watching the light change, listening to the ever-so-slightly-shifting sounds that signal the next step in the cyclical process of forest life. Other times, I sit on the threshold's edge and watch the bees instead.

My deck is an ecosystem all on its own. There is not a single matching planting pot, and I have a robust collection of rocks, bricks, chairs and tables, as well as a strange variety of plants. Herbs are planted in this pot and that, as well as in this other hanging one—thyme, rosemary, flat-leaf Italian parsley, oregano, lemon balm, green chives, dill and basil. Creeping Jenny trails down the sides of larger terracotta pots, while yellow rose bushes, small and proud, are stationed at each corner of the second-storey landing. I've acquired day-lilies and black-eyed Susan, Stargazer lilies, French lavender and orange kalanchoe. Experimentation and curiosity have landed me three avocado trees, as well as a lemon tree. The most glorious of the collection, though, and the reason for such abundant availability of bee watching, are the ever-expanding and extraordinarily hardy and drought resistant pink-flowering Autumn Joy sedum.

These little bunches of star-shaped florals fork out from several nodes. Each junction is upheld by a single tall, lanky, deep-pink stalk with a tower of offset, rounded olive-green leaves climbing all the way up. In a pot, connected to one bunch of roots, could be ten to fifteen stalks, all bearing a variety of nodes and a bunch of tiny flowers at the top. I started with one set of bulbs in a single pot and have since expanded to seven, each year needing to split the plant into more pots for optimal health. Native to some parts of North America, this plant is a pollinating magnet. I can sit for hours watching the comings and goings of bees, flies, butterflies, dragonflies and the occasional wasp, counting ten, twelve, twenty winged buzzers at a single pot. Like staring into the wobble of a flame, it's easy to be lost in the busy world of these bugs—easy enough to not notice the spider and her web, strung up in some unlucky flier's path. Alongside life and abundance is brutality.

Some falls are filled with the right amount of rain: there is moisture in the air, enough for the soil and plants and bugs. Other falls are not so lucky. One fall in recent memory, the rain was all out of whack. It just did not come. The summer had been hot—thankfully not heat dome hot—and the fall began with glorious warm weather. We frolicked later into the year than I had ever frolicked before, enjoying every moment of the extended summer. Typically, by the middle of October, our wood fireplace is on, the windows are closed and we, like the rest of the active forest, are busy preparing for the winter ahead. But during the autumn that the rain did not come there was so much suffering throughout the natural world: across the province, water required for salmon runs and successful spawning dried up, leaving thousands of suffocating fish scattered along empty creek beds. The forest and my back deck grew quiet. Fewer bees buzzed. Spiders did not take up camp on my deck. Plants and trees struggled as they slipped slowly into comas, not growing or changing the way their cycle demands. They quietly died instead, sliding into decay without the life that typically accompanies natural transitions. It was a poignant comparison to us frolicking humans.

That dry October, there was something different about the broadleaf maple trees in the mountains, along the city streets and scattered throughout city parks. Rather than their typical vibrant display of orange, yellow and red—or even dead-brown like during the heat dome year—the leaves were a dull silvery-grey. I couldn't account for their lack of pigmentation. That glorious transitional phase was simply not there.

Confused, I went in search of answers. I wandered into the woods and studied the maples. I scrutinized their front side and their backside, their stems and branches. I inspected the bark and the roots and earth around them, looking for fungus and other signs of decay. I brought my face close to low hanging leaves, nose nearly touching. There, I saw the plague infecting these trees: the leaves were white. I pinched the corner of one. A gritty powder rubbed off on my thumb and index finger. I smelled it—as all good inspectors do. Mildew. I looked up and realized that every single maple in the vicinity of where I stood had leaves just like this one. They were pale, stiff and covered in powdery white. Sickly. Devastated. Utterly colourless. All of them.

I thought back to the summer and remembered briefly thinking that it was odd that Sumas Mountain appeared dull and silvery when I looked up at it from the valley, although I hadn't thought much of it. Why didn't I see it? Why hadn't I noticed? That fall, the white leaves were all I could see.

I discovered that the broadleaf maples were afflicted with a fungal parasite that turns their foliage and stems white as snow. The cause for the spread of this white powder is stress on the trees, including excessive and prolonged heat, massive flooding and heavy winds. I was told by many different people that what I was seeing was only cosmetic and would not cause any long-term harm, but I couldn't help but wonder whether this was a short-sighted point of view. What happens when this fungus comes back every year? What happens when the trees continue to be stressed, over and over? Will this not weaken the population of trees over time? How is this not something to be concerned about?

When I was small, my father would send me to the basement to fetch some tool he needed to mend a fence or a tractor or the door of a horse stall. I'd race across the yard, muttering to myself over and over what it was he had asked for, trying desperately to avoid forgetting. I'd reach the back of the house and start down the four concrete steps leading to a sunken landing and the door to our underground basement. I would remind myself to walk slowly down these steps; from time to time, a Pacific giant salamander or two may be stranded in the concrete desert.

I got in the habit of checking for Sally, which became the name for every salamander I saw. It seemed that I'd often be running to recruit help because I'd spotted Sally and she needed to be rescued. Making sure our cat was inside, my father and I would return to the stairwell, and I'd watch as the salamander was gently scooped up into my father's large palm. Sometimes she would protest with the tiniest throaty growl as we relocated her to the dampness of a nearby creek, where we hoped she would moisten up a bit, eat and make a home.

We did our best to watch out for the salamanders who became trapped; the coolness of the below-ground-level cement and dampness that seemed to never go away, no matter the season, appeared to attract them. Once they managed to find themselves there, though, I am not sure whether they could get out on their own. More than once, we found a shrivelled Sally hiding in the corner, dry and starved. More than once, one of the many roaming neighbourhood cats has walked off with one. In building this house on this land in the way we did, we had unintentionally created our own version of a spider's trap—except that this trap wasn't part of the ecosystem. It wasn't part of the give and take, the cycle of regeneration. It was all take. Over the years, I saw Sally less and less until one day I forgot all about her. We haven't seen a salamander anywhere on our property for many years. The moisture levels natural to this area have continued to decrease. This is my burden, one of my many burdens, as I participate in the slow decimation of biodiverse ecosystems.

My parents taught me as a young girl to watch out for wild-life on the roads. I was a dutiful passenger then and I try my best to be a dutiful driver now. Squirrels will dart out into the street and stop in a panic in the middle of the road, tail stick-ing straight up in the air, and then continue to the other side or turn back, understanding they had made a grave mistake. Birds will jump about the road, picking at roadkill, collect-ing bugs or cracking nuts on the hard asphalt. They most often move before a car gets close, but sometimes they don't. Deer will lurk in the bushes and ditches, nearly invisible and blending into the scenery with exquisite ease, then leap out and freeze, standing there wide eyed as your vehicle comes barrelling toward it.

One afternoon in the early fall some years ago, just as the first trees were changing from green to yellow and the mountain saw the sun grow lower each day, I exchanged my walking shoes for a set of tires as I left the mountain to meet a friend for coffee. With each drive to town in recent years, the cars on the roads had noticeably increased in volume, one effect of the many new housing developments. Naturally, with the increase of cars comes the increase of careless driv-ers, and this means less careful attention to whatever could be lurking on the threshold between road and forest. It is becoming more difficult to separate wildlife habitat from hu-man habitat.

Midway through my route, several cars were parked alongside the road. At first glance, there seemed to be no reason why they should be there. Then, someone stepped out of their vehicle. Tall and lanky, he loped his way into the middle of the road. Though he watched for cars coming from both directions, his intentions were set at reaching a large body lying in the street. There was a buck, a young blacktail deer, small antlers and all. He had been struck by one of the parked vehicles. I pulled off the road onto the leaf-covered gravel shoulder and watched. The deer was still alive. He arched his neck, wide-eyed in desperation, as the tall man approached. One free leg pawed slowly at the air. I wanted to get out of the car, I wanted to help him return home, but no other part of the deer moved. I knew his legs were broken. The patch of road beneath him was darkened by too much blood and it was likely that he was bleeding internally as well. The deer was caught unaware and struck down. In the distance, a conservation officer's vehicle was coming up the road. There was nothing I could do.

I pulled back onto the street, crunching shoulder gravel and autumn leaves beneath each tire. I slowly carried on. The deer and his terrified eyes grew smaller in my rear-view mirror, and then faded altogether.

WALKING WITH GIANTS

One morning in early fall, I went for a walk with John Vissers, a young sixty-something neighbour who has seen me through all the stages of my life. Here and there, scattered amongst second- and third-growth trees on Sumas Mountain, old-growth trees still stand, silent and stoic, and we were going to look for them.

John lives across the street from me, third house on the right. The Vissers bought their land in the eighties and refused to bring in fill to build up the property, so the area still feels a little wild. From the street the house is hidden; it is surrounded by moss- and lichen-covered trees, slender cedars, proud firs, sprawling vines and thick broad leaf maples. Moss sticks to cedar bark and looks like tiny ferns. The lichen hanging from fir tree branches dangles in your face as you walk by and everywhere your foot wants to step, over fallen trees and around accumulated earth, are vast and thick green carpets made of countless types of moss: liverwort, ragged, broom, sickle, step, leafy, feather, haircap, knights plume and cat's tail. The marshy pond at the back of the property and undergrowth everywhere produce a soft quietude that permeates the senses of any visitor willing to pay attention.

On that misty cool Sunday morning in early October, fog hanging low in the trees, my Chevrolet Bolt electric car and I collected John at the mouth of his driveway. With a slight wiry build and hair that seems whiter with each greeting, John is an unassuming character with an incomparable wealth of knowledge of Sumas Mountain. It had rained profusely all night and we anticipated that it would rain again that day. Like any good West Coaster, we go into the woods anyhow. Clad with rain jackets, hats and backpacks full of snacks and water, we set off.

From Charlie Spruce Place, we take a left at the stop sign and coast down Dawson Road to the four-way intersection, where Dawson meets Sumas Mountain Road. To the left is a new subdivision, sitting on land that once housed both a bright yellow one-room schoolhouse and a stonemason's home and business. The schoolhouse was built in the early 1900s in what would become Straiton Village, when settlers came to the area after clay had been found. Small communities—like Straiton Village, as well as Kilgard, Clayburn and Heritage Valley—popped up around the mountain. Straiton Village became a collection of large homesteads, a post office, general store, school and community centre, participating in the early twentieth century's significant transformation of Sumas Mountain, a sacred place for the Semá:th People of the Sumas First Nation.

Today, Straiton Community Hall, the last building left from the early 1900s, stands among a series of subdivisions, an oil refinery and a gravel mine. The developers named the street going into that new subdivision Diane Brooke. I am told it is named after the creek running in the ditch alongside Dawson Road. Who is Diane? What legacy does her name erase?

At the four-way intersection John and I turn right, heading north up Sumas Mountain Road. The road winds along a crest in the mountainside, going up, up, up, then turns downward at a steep decline on the north side, over-looking the Fraser River and Mission in the distance. The road turns to gravel. We drive slowly down the backside of the mountain and then pull a U-turn where the road widens at one side and park along the northwest edge, the nose of the car facing up toward where we had come.

Before Sumas Mountain Road became a road for ve-hicles, it was called Wades Trail. Even before that, it was an important route for the Semá:th People who lived, hunted and traded in the area. This path was the only way to get from the Fraser River to the Sumas Border during certain months: the surrounding area, what is now Sumas Prairie on one side, Matsqui Prairie on the other and Abbotsford in between, was wetland and lake. Before dikes, drainage systems and pumps were built to make the land suitable for farming and devel-opment, the river flooded each year, making the base of the mountain entirely impassable. What is now Sumas Mountain Road was one of the only routes that wound from one side of the mountain to the other.

Slinging our packs across our backs, crossing the road from where we parked, John and I step over the threshold from the gravel road onto the path. Built in 1967, the trail-head of the Centennial Trail was originally near the base of the mountain. It was the project of retired loggers and locals, eager to create a path that made it easy to appreciate the spectacular beauty of this area. Time, circumstances, tree lots, logging, purchasing of land and the creation of park boundaries caused the route to change over time. It went out of service for many years until it was rerouted, becoming the path that John and I are venturing onto. Today, the trail avoids some unsafe sections that once took hikers past Lover's Leap and other deadly cliffs. Much of the trail, though, still follows the original logging roads that led to Chadsey Lake, known by some as Lost Lake. The trees were once all so massive, some measuring fifty feet around, that when originally logged, way before my time, they were driven down the mountain one tree at a time.

We pass a notice indicating there are bears and sensitive habitats in the area. A metal box is stationed on a post with a counter inside, tracking the number of users entering this area each day. We cross the threshold and into the woods, instantly enveloped by the moist air only a temperate rainforest in fall can offer. What a difference this breath makes. How unimaginable and distant the summer heat seemed now.

Marching up Sumas Mountain with John is a bit like tracking into a wild place with a mythical creature. His words are filled with wisdom and colour. My mind relaxes as we begin to walk through the deep green and fiery orange of a forest that looks painted. The mountain is above, below and under us. I breathe in the drizzling October air, heavy with misty particles that feel as ancient as the area itself. The ground is soggy and sends mud outwards beneath our feet with each step we take, leaving an outline of our boot prints. Water trickles down the path in many places. Although we wear smart footwear, we know our feet will be damp by the end of our adventure. We don't mind: we are looking for a patch of old-growth trees, part of the less than 2 percent of old growth left standing in all of BC. Wet feet are an after-thought. This is the way these forests are supposed to be.

John is animated with excitement as we cross a wide bridge over a tumultuous October creek. He tells of the day he and a group of researchers found a red-tailed frog there. "We didn't think we'd find any!" he exclaims. "It was right over there." He points to the south side of the water's edge, across from where we stand on the bridge. Sumas is also home to a collection of unique creatures.

John tells me that the mountain's microclimate sits at the northern edge of a larger and more biodiverse area home to many species. The edge of a species' bubble is where the most genetic diversity exists, allowing multiple species to be collectively healthy. "These are what we call keystone spe-cies," John says, in his usual colourful tone, as we step off the bridge and back onto the wet and narrow footpath.

"The problem arises," he says, turning his shoulders slightly to talk to me as we continue up the trail, "when the edges of a large biosphere start to fall." This could be due to climate change, invasive species or general human existence. "Over time," he continues, "a new edge falls, and another, and then another." On and on it goes until an entire species and those dependent upon it tumble like dominoes.

"The remnant we have here is," he continues, "well, it's

irreplaceable. It gives you a sense of space, of what it would have been like. We need to keep a remnant to remind us of what this area should look like or what it could look like, or what it might again someday look like." Without a connection to the past, through old-growth forests or patches of land left untouched or a mountain left alone and allowed to be a mountain without stripping its life force for someone else's profit, how will we ever know what we have lost? How will we ever know what could be?

John's passion for this place gives me pause. I wonder what it was like where we are walking now, at the tip of Sumas Mountain, before the Centennial Trail was built, before the loggers and settlers and miners arrived. I look around as we hike, listening to the branches gently rubbing against each other in the wind and the delicate trickling waterways— the whispers of the forest. With each step, I feel as if I am growing heavier with memory. I see the past through the wet, foggy air closing in around us as we ascend.

This vision of the past sees soft earth with minimal ground cover. The canopy of trees is so high above me that a feeling of spaciousness permeates my perspective. This openness reaches outward and upward from the base of tall, straight and wide-footed trees crowded by numerous varieties of ferns, mosses, lichen and fungus plugging into the network that begins deep underground in a tangle of roots. The network behaves like a single organism that helps the ecosystem above it breathe and grow as one. Above ground, that reaching canopy lets golden light shine through the treetops, lighting up the multi-shaded green and turning everything into jewels. An inhale through the nose, an exhale out the mouth: the air is misty and cool in my lungs. There is no end to the reach of this old-growth forest, as communities of trees are bound to each other beneath the ground, in the canopy and in the space in-between. The only sounds are the rustling of ferns, the chirping call of birds, the hoot of an owl, the *thud, thud* of a bear crashing through the undergrowth and the scurrying of red squirrels. This is an old-growth forest. This is what John and I have come to find in the shadows of logged areas on Sumas Mountain.

About an hour into our hike, John and I pause at a bend. The trail goes east. We are headed west, off trail, to find the grove of ancient trees. I take a long drink of water, and then we gingerly step off the path, careful not to disturb the undergrowth. We take two separate routes through ferns, around rocks, past stumps and fallen debris. John continues to tell stories. He talks briefly about the difference between old-growth forests, planted forests and logged forests that have been given time and space to repopulate. Most of Sumas Mountain's second- or third-growth forests were allowed to return on their own. In doing this, the production of a monoculture forest is avoided. This is a forest subsisting of only one type of tree, becoming much like a cornfield where biodiversity is largely non-existent. The trees in a monoculture aren't as healthy as other forests. Like the falling edges of a biosphere, the area lacks the diversity necessary to protect it from disease, pests and forest fires.

At the crest of a small hill, the path fades away behind us; before us lies entry into another world. Thousands of healthy sword ferns fan out across the earth; they've had space and time to thrive. As I step among them, I find it difficult to know where the ferns end and the ground begins. I walk slowly, following John's confident lead, fearing my boot may discover a hole and I'd be lost forever in this strange transitional terrain.

Beyond the ferny plateau, someone has cut down a bigleaf maple; its burl has been poached and the tree left for dead, an unfortunate and common occurrence in forests across BC. This body marks the gateway into a world I am drawn into. There, in the near distance, a dozen Douglas fir trees, the grandmothers of a forgotten world. A profound silence permeates this space, quieting my heart and my mind, taking up residence throughout my body.

As I step into a depression in the earth surrounded by the looming sentinels, I note how the mountain changes. The light filters differently. The mist settles slightly askew, its particles drifting in a hardly perceptible breeze. The canopy above is vast while the foliage below is open and airy: there are no brambles to walk over and around. There are no stumps or debris. There is no thicket blocking our way. I close my eyes and breathe. The sweet scent of fall, decaying leaves, damp moss and a cooling air synesthetically pervade every sense available to me. I feel at once out of place and at home, as if I'd passed a threshold into a time that is both mine and not mine. I feel the presence of the Douglas firs so absolutely, even with my eyes closed.

I ask John why it feels so good to be here. Why do I feel so rested and at peace? Why, regardless of effort, am I never quite at ease in the same way anywhere else? "Cultural experience versus natural experience," he says. Perhaps we are instinctively hard wired to feel good in the forest. "You can't stand next to a tree like this," he continues, his gaze climbing the massive trunk, "and not feel some kind of emotion." He goes quiet for a moment, his head tilted, before explaining that in experiencing this place, we have an opportunity to remember there are other ways of being. We can see that trees are not like us, but maybe we can learn to be more like them. Maybe we can learn to be a stronger community, to work together, to help each other grow while taking lessons from the remnants of the past.

Despite the spitting rain, foggy ground and my damp feet, on this October Sunday the overwhelming beauty of the forest is astounding. The grove of remaining giants left behind—because they were too small to log, because the loggers already had what they wanted or maybe because the Great Depression hit and these trees were no longer worth the trouble—still stands quietly. They are remnants of an ephemeral time, a time I believe I can feel when I raise my hand to the bark of an ancient cedar and close my eyes. A time nonetheless that I will never know. Situated far back from the path well taken, I hope these groves remain forgotten. On our descent and all the way home John and I talk a little less.

Each morning, as fall slowly descends into winter and the deciduous trees lose their leaves, exposing the grey branches beneath, I sit at my writing desk and try to take in the peace and beauty of this mountain. I try to imagine and engage with the remnant of what was, but I am often shaken by the slow growl of growth that never seems to quit: from my house, I can hear the rock quarry digging into the lungs of the mountain. They blast. Louder. Louder. Louder. The house shakes; glasses *ting, ting, ting*. Silence for a moment, then their machines continue to grind and crunch and move about on the broken face of this place. It could almost be confused with the crashing of waves, although we are far from the ocean and upon closer consideration, there is nothing peaceful about the beeping of trucks, growling of machines and blasting of rock.

The trail behind our property can lead me to an edge of the forest that falls open to the rock quarry. A great, expansive grey filters into the muted sky above, which reaches, bends above me and folds into the empty arms of newly naked branches behind me. The more this mountain is dug up and carted away in the name of progress, the larger the chasm between what was and what is, what could be.

BIRDS OF PARADISE

From time to time, in the early mornings of late fall, the owls' *hoo-hoo*s dominate the woods once again as they did in spring. Early morning *hoo-hoo*s often turn into a long, drawn out and deeply toned *hoooooooo, hoooooo* on one side of our property, which is responded to by a faster-paced and higher-pitched *hoo-hoo* from the opposite direction. The two holler at each other, with slight changes in the length and tone of each *hoo*. Owl speak.

Sometimes it is a gentle *hoo-hoo* conversation between two. Other times it is the shriek of a kill or a warning to other predators. I love to listen and try to decipher the events around these calls. When the dawn is still a time away, I grab a blanket and creep outside. I sit in the grass or in the moss under a tree and listen in the crisp autumn air to a conversation in a language I'll never know. I want to hear these birds speak as often as I can for as long as I can.

Later, when I step onto the trails of Sumas Mountain during those seasonal changes, exercising a keen eye at the right time of day, I might see one of the owls, sometimes two if I'm lucky. They sit patiently in the treed canopy, watching and waiting for the scurrying of a land critter rustling a set of leaves below. The birds always anticipate the perfect opportunity to seize lunch.

The owl is sensitive to the environment around her; she feels the air move and senses the slight shift of the light as dusk approaches. She watches the ground with incredible sight, simultaneously observing the entirety of the forest from a safe and careful perch in a Douglas fir tree near her burrow some distance away. She is extraordinarily beautiful and her soft feathers, with their gradient grey and brown colouring, help her merge with the wooded tapestry. She is creative in where she perches, where she looks and how she swoops toward her prey. She is planning for a particular result with great focus. She is in direct competition with other creatures, winged or not, so she must be smart. There is a precise aggression as she dives to catch an unsuspecting mouse nuzzling its food along the forest floor. There is experience and skill in her waiting and watching, the swoop and kill.

These birds are one of many species that populate Sumas Mountain and the Fraser Valley each year. In the spring, owls arrive with swallows, hummingbirds, ravens, chickadees, red-headed woodpeckers, red-breasted sapsuckers, the hermit thrush, the warbler, peregrine falcons, trumpeter swans and Canada geese. They arrive in a gossipy flurry, seemingly all at once. When autumn rolls around, only some of these birds will stay to weather the winter. Others, as quickly as they arrived, begin preparation for their great migration.

One afternoon, I was walking along Clayburn Road. Sumas Mountain was in front of me to the east, towering in the distance; Mission and the Fraser River were to the north, beyond the valley's farmland; to the south were the remaining wetlands of Matsqui Flats and Sumas Prairie just before the United States; and much farther west lay Vancouver and the coast. Suddenly a flock of Canada geese resting in the field of drying wheat next to the road got my attention. They became excited. Like a large family attempting to leave the house on a weekday morning, they were all in motion, waddling about, honking, tail feathers wiggling. Then, as if rehearsed a thousand times, liftoff—all at once, they took to the skies.

The leader of the flock, aiming for the peak of the mountain, struck a steep precedent. The remainder of the birds worked hard to match. Up, up, up and forward they went, deeper into Clayburn Village and closer to the base of the mountain. Some lagged; some fell out of formation before correcting and aligning themselves back into place. Birds rotated, back to front, front to back, middle crossing over middle. The form seems to be alive as it shifts and sways, widens, and narrows, slows and speeds up. The flock moves like a single organism as each goose takes its turn as the lead. It was as smooth and seamless as the changing colours of a clear sky at sundown.

I watched as the V-formation headed toward the mountain until, as if they had reached a satisfactory height, it turned right. Led by the goose at the tip of the V, the birds curved around and headed back in the direction from which they'd come. Back toward me. My slow saunter down Clayburn Road slowed until I stood, awed, as the flock came nearer and lower, a steady beat of wings and sharp black beaks pointing the way, communicating with a deafening cacophony of honks as they went. I gawked as they flew over me, flashing their underbellies, then turned again to come soaring down to earth, landing in the field adjacent to the road, the same place they had taken off. I felt as though they had just completed a successful test flight.

Where I stood that day, at the western base of Sumas Mountain in what is now Clayburn Village, was once all wetland. When dykes were created and Sumas Lake was drained, the wetland areas that expanded and shrunk with the seasons all but disappeared. But if I wander there and open my imagination, sometimes I can picture what might have been.

Varieties of semi-aquatic tall and short grasses and reeds, sedges and shrubs cover any area not completely submerged by open shallow waters, creating natural canals, ponds and marshes of various depths. The ground is soft and sandy and I imagine water squishing out from underneath my boots. Pockets of evergreen and deciduous trees appear here and there, growing denser the farther east they go until they seamlessly blend with those ancient firs and cedars on Sumas Mountain.

Thickets of easy places to hide and nest and varieties of mosquitos and flies, dragonflies and beetles, frogs and crickets, spiders and butterflies make wetlands like this a haven for all manner of flying creatures. Nesting on land and in these grasses and bushes, I imagine thriving killdeers, plump little marsh wrens, pied-billed grebes and the common snipe.

In more open waters, rafts of mallards, gaggles of geese and banks of swans gather in a cacophony of paddling, honking, quacking and gurgling. Their flipper feet and legs hidden beneath the surface of the water help them glide around in teams of various sizes and speeds. I watch as in my mind's eye they mostly stay within their own troupe but coexist with one another peacefully. A lone heron or pelican is standing near the water's edge, one leg tucked underneath, while in tall trees nearby giant eagles and falcons and ravens watch over the chaos below.

In the winter, mallards stand on orange-and-black webbed palmate feet in areas that have been frozen over, their heads and necks hunched into winged shoulders. Others glide peacefully in the water not-yet frozen over until someone decides it's time to get wet: down goes a beak, up go the tail feathers. Meanwhile, proud white swans with long necks and thick bodies move across large spaces in these waters. When it's time to take off, their white-and-black heads bob up and down, wings stretch outward and begin their enormous flapping. Their necks stretch forward as they use all their might to lift their bodies into the air, water splashing in their wake and then settling for other water-loving birds to move through. In spite of spring mosquitos and summer flies, this place would have been breathtaking.

There is a remnant of this past in Willband Creek Park, a nearby protected area. Created in 1990, this park began as flood control after an area close by was cleared, paved and developed: without trees to hold the water in the ground, rains and streams ran off into Clayburn Village. After some time passed, this area became an obvious place to help support the health of the remaining wetlands. A sign at the entrance, with art created by local naturalist Glenn Ryder, showcases the great variety of birds who need this place to survive. Bird and duck boxes and bat houses and osprey platforms have been installed to support vulnerable species. But is this small slice, afflicted by invasive plant species, next to a busy highway, across from a noisy train track and surrounded by housing and subdivisions, plopped in the centre of a growing city, enough to protect the vulnerable populations that exist here? What will climate change do to the moisture in these wetlands? How will air, light or water pollution impact the insects these creatures depend on? How will this ecosystem stand up against the encroaching world?

And yet—whenever I visit Willband, no matter the season, it is always filled with action: during the day, geese, swans and ducks are busy and animated; and at night, bats and owls emerge to take advantage of a quieter sky.

ONE, TWO, TREE

Wandering up Sumas Mountain one day, I found myself in an area I had been many times before. It started with a drive up Sumas Mountain Road, down Batt Road, then a sharp right when the asphalt turns to gravel. Pass through the yellow iron gate and follow the kilometre markers up a short way to a clearing: Sumas Mountain Provincial Park. As I crested the hill, expecting to see tall trees and soft earthen ground beneath, anticipating a cool and quiet walk in the woods, what greeted me instead was a hot, brown cutblock. I could still smell the sticky sweet sap, like very mild sugar water, a wonderful scent that doesn't match the harsh image of a barren logged forest. I parked the car and stepped outside to examine this new naked mountainside.

The trees were gone. What remained was a collection of stumps still red from where the saw blade had cut into them. It wasn't just one or two trees here and there; it was an entire section of the forest. What had been cool, damp and filled with life was now barren. I could see the valley to the south and west; I could walk among the decimated and the dead. I stood in the clearing and remained there, waiting to hear the sounds I had initially come to the park to hear. It was as if the mountain had been stunned into a pervading silence. The only sound I heard was the howl of a new kind of wind no longer meeting resistance from the thick forest that once was there.

As a kid, I had come to this section of the mountain from time to time with my family. We'd walk through the trees and spy the birds, squirrels and deer. Here, I learned to watch out for mushrooms and step around delicate foliage. I discovered the scent of the woods—the variations between sappy pine, warm cedar, musty maple leaves and damp soil, and the sweetness of dew early in the morning. The fullness of a still-treed forest with its myriad of smells is such a contrast to the singular misleading sweetness when an entire chunk of the woods goes missing. But even in a cutblock—with the sun beaming down, when the fullness that I have grown so used to is no longer there, and I miss that feeling of comfort and familiarity when I walk among tall trees—there is still something to discover, some new perspective to behold and a chance to see with fresh eyes.

When the sun shines between the stumps of a cut-block, it casts a different set of shadows—low and fat. This draws my attention to the earth around that stump: I can no longer gaze into the treed canopy, so I gaze down instead. The stump itself, freshly sawed, is red and raw. The surface is jagged and rough. When I touch it, a wetness seeps out from the sore and onto my hand, which I use to trace down the sides all the way to the earth below. Near the base, all manner of bugs have been unearthed: beetles, black spiders and, if we are at the right time of year, various species of caterpillars that will turn into moths and butterflies—if they aren't picked off by circling birds first.

With my head low to the ground, surveying the earth and looking out at the expanse of stumps fanning out around me, I am overwhelmed at the sweet, warm scent emitted from the stump, the ground and the left-over shavings from when the saw cut into the tree. The ground is covered with these shavings, sprinkling the trampled foliage that weaves around the stumps.

There is a scent somewhere nearby that brings me back to the tenth grade: gym class, archery. The teacher would line everyone up, give us a bow and three cedar arrows and, one at a time, we drew and loosed those arrows toward our target. Inevitably, someone would step on an arrow and break it or crack it on purpose just for fun and a strong cedar scent would fill the gymnasium. Those arrows had been made from dried wood. Now, standing in a freshly cut forest and moved by the memory of that cedar sweetness, I came to realize that although I wished the forest was still intact, and although I wished I could walk among the tall trees and feel comforted and enclosed by them, believing they would remain there for hundreds of years, there is something nonetheless strangely beautiful about this newly opened landscape. The sun hits it differently, casting different shadows. Its scents are sweeter and more powerful. The sky is open and welcoming, and I can look out into the vista and into the valley below in a way that I never could before. I struggle with the loss and with acknowledging the beauty I see.

Of course, this fresh, wounded beauty will change

again: the coral-red stumps, their delicious scent and the new shadows they cast, along with the bugs teeming around them, will transform. The stumps will become a dull brown and the saccharine scent will give way to earthiness. As winter grows near, the shadows will grow smaller; but as the foliage around the stumps extends upwards to the open sky, other new shadows will grow longer. The bugs in this wide-open space will provide fodder for the birds and bats. The cutblock is emblematic of the contradictions that come with change.

The summer of my nineteenth birthday, I folded a tent, shovel and red duffel bag into the trunk of my black 1993 Honda Civic sedan. Destination: BC's interior to plant trees for the summer. Armed with rain gear, planting bags, hot pink flagging tape, gloves and bug spray, I hit the highway out of Abbotsford, headlights pointed toward Prince George.

I'd heard rumours of the amount of money a tree planter could make if they were quick on their feet and efficient with a shovel. As an undergrad going into my last year of study, uncertain of what my next step would be, a summer accumulating cash sounded like the perfect plan. Casting away the idealized version of my summer vacation, coming to terms with the logging industry and trying to learn how to become a tree planter was an experience unto itself. I'm not sure I ever really got there; I'm not sure I ever became one.

While other planters were counting boxes of trees they had put in the ground and calculating the profit accumulated that day, proud of the amount of terrain they'd covered, how straight their roots were and whether they thought they'd heard a grizzly tussling about near the edge of the logged block, I was thinking about glyphosate, the spray provided by forestry companies and aerially spread across cutblocks like the one where I was. It can kill any underbrush attempting to take hold of the land. Some forestry companies claim that the spray makes it easier for seedlings to grow as they won't compete with other root systems, although environmental scientists and ecologists refute this, suggesting glyphosate causes more long-term harm to forests and ecosystems. I was also too preoccupied with the slash piles.

Whenever a chunk of treed land is logged, there is a certain amount of timber that isn't seen as valuable for production and doesn't get loaded up and trucked out. Those cut trees are left in massive piles sometimes twenty feet high. The logging companies were following government guidelines and policies—these large slash piles were permitted—but this waste, or what seemed like waste to me, weighed heavy on my mind during those months as a planter, first in Prince George, then Chetwynd and finally in Tumbler Ridge. I was in mourning.

Of course, my own family on Sumas Mountain has logged much of our five acres to put in a field to raise horses and chickens and goats and children, so my aversion to tree planting initially surprised me. In addition, trees continued to come down throughout my childhood and into adulthood as the wood-burning stove in my parents' house acted as the major heat source. I loved the dry warmth of the wood stove. Picking the tree we were to fell was a careful process. We wandered about the property, selecting the ones that were in danger of coming down on their own or were in direct competition with the growth of another. We never selected a mother tree; Professor of Forest Ecology Susan Simard's research has shown that old trees can be connected to the forest through complex fungal networks below ground, and that this communication provides crucial nutrients to seedlings. Respect was evident in our decision-making process. Once we picked the right tree, I loved the felling process, chopping wood and stacking it in the shed, tossing each quartered log from one set of gloved hands to another and then another, down the family assembly line. We used as much of the tree as possible and felled as few as we could. I loved tidying up the excess branches and small logs and figuring out what to make out of the extra parts. Those extra parts became walking sticks and wreaths and strange bookshelves in my childhood bedroom; they transformed into blocks for new nieces and nephews, coasters for Christmas presents, a side table in my barn house, picture frames on every wall and cutting boards stacked on the kitchen counter.

Any time a tree came down in the neighbourhood, it seemed that everyone came out to watch. My father, nearly always at the helm, had turned into a strange sort of celebrity. Everyone loved to see Rick take out a tree, his showmanship and precision. In front of his audience, he'd set himself up near the selected tree and then examine it carefully. He considered the possible weight of its branches and any widow-makers barely hanging off the trunk, ready to fall onto an unsuspecting passerby. He checked to see whether any part was rotting, checking for mushrooms around the base, or if the slope of the hill would make felling difficult. He designated a path that he would send the sentinel down as it was felled, determining where the tip should land so as not to disturb any other structure, natural or man-made. He moved with a strong, kind assuredness.

One fall, the bigleaf maple near the front of the property had been dropping its branches, showing serious evidence of decay. My family selected it for felling. On a Sunday morning, after breakfast and coffee were consumed, Dad headed out in his orange-collared fleece jacket, yellow reflector strips on the back and wrapping around both arms. The birds were chirping and the sun had just cracked through the clouds; it was a warm September Sunday.

Before getting geared up with boots, spikes, a harness and earplugs, Dad walked around the tree. He glanced up at the trunk, tilted his head to one side, muttered to himself, then wandered to the other side. Eyes up again. Head tilted. He continued to circle, inspecting the base of the tree from this angle and that, touching the bark here and there, applying pressure and releasing. He stepped heavily, with purpose, on the earth, then watched for any movement of the surrounding trees. He would walk away from the maple, stop, turn and look up at it again; there was something like choreography in his movements. At this point, the audience was just my mother, brother, sister and me. When people were around, Dad began verbalizing every thought. Growing up, I always felt that he was speaking to the tree, asking it questions, making claims and explanations, but he was almost always just talking to himself in our general direction. Regardless, his prattle and action-driven attitude inevitably drew people not only into the conversation, but into the intense drama of the business of felling a tree.

Once satisfied with his assessment of the maple, Dad limbed a few branches. Then, clad with spikes attached to his boots and strapped to a harness connected to the body of the tree like a sling, he moved up the trunk. His chainsaw was attached to a rope hanging from a clasp on his harness.

Step, step, shimmy the harness up.

Step, step, shimmy the harness up.

Reaching the first branch, he pulled up the rope attached to the chainsaw, yanked on the throttle of the gas motor, and cut into the first of the widow-makers. It broke from the tree with a crack and thudded heavily to the earth below. Several shrivelled leaves let go with the force and fluttered downward, chasing their host.

Step, step, shimmy the harness up.

This went on until there were no dangerous branches left. He made his way back down to earth with this part of the job finished. By this point, more than a few neighbours had appeared and were gawking at the spectacle, drawn by the chainsaw's racket.

Happy to have an audience, and feet on the earth once more, Dad chatted with everyone. Proudly, he claimed he'd be able to have the tree land exactly where he wanted it to, not one inch to the left or right, and that it would not so much as tickle any other plant or structure. It would be a clean fall, he assured them. The neighbours looked at the land around the tree, glancing sideways at one another. Directly to the left was the house; directly to the right was a white fence enclosing the field, horses and a patch of other trees. In front was the vegetable garden and more fence. Looking up once more at the mammoth maple, the neighbours decided that it could not be done. Even if it fell exactly where he wanted, surely the top would be in the garden.

Unphased, Dad tied a thick yellow rope around the base of the tree. Below that rope, he made cuts into the trunk. He went in about a foot, then backed out. Then, he used the chainsaw to measure a length, moved up about eight inches from the original cut, shifted the saw to a forty-five-degree angle and cut into the bark again. He went back and forth between the two cuts a few times until he was satisfied. Then, he put down the saw and picked up the sledgehammer.

With a few hefty swings, a chunk of maple blew out of the trunk, leaving behind a gap ten inches high and as wide as the trunk itself. Next, he checked to see that the rope was fastened tightly around the circumference of the tree above the severed section. He dragged the loose end in the direction he wanted the maple to fall, then made his way to the backside, away from the gap.

He announced his calculations to his audience, building up the drama. Soon, the crowd had grown from seven or eight viewers to fifteen, steaming cups of coffee in hand and cameras at the ready. Then, Dad decided it was time. He and the tree were ready.

Since he had a considerable number of willing viewers, he decided to put two of them to work. He explained that he was going to cut *here*, pointing to one side of the trunk, and the two volunteers would stand *there*, pointing to where he had placed the end of the rope, the place he predicted where the tip of the tree would land. After the cutting began, he instructed them, and the tree started to creak, they should pull on the rope to encourage the tree to fall in the right place. Then, with an air of mischief, he told the audience and his volunteers that if the tree looks like it might land on them, they should run. He started up the gas motor of the chainsaw once again—*Bruuhhh brh brh brh brh brrrrrrrreeeeeee!* The saw screamed as it bit into the back of the maple. Sawdust blew in all directions. The mixture of chainsaw gas, grease and the sweetness of fresh timber exfoliated the air, a slight breeze coaxing the scent toward each witness.

Suddenly, the tree began to sway. The tippy top leaned one way, then another. Leaves in the branches quivered. *Pull!* The two volunteers pulled, then stepped aside. It seemed as though a silence pervaded the whole area; even the fall birds in the neighbouring trees stalled their chatter as the great sentinel creaked and leaned, and then with a sudden *whoosh*, crashed down, shuddering the earth we stood on.

The maple was on the ground precisely where Dad had said it would be. There was applause and cheers, and cans of beer came out of two or three pockets and were cracked open and slammed together to toast the occasion.

We inspected the deep rot at the centre of the tree and measured the rings of the stump. This tree was over eighty years old and had endured years of both drought and high water; it had seen heavy stress and easy days. Dad invited the neighbours to pick up an axe or a chainsaw and help him chip away at the timber. Some stayed, happy to participate, while the others thanked him for the show and wandered back to their lives.

Over the next few days, I helped my family stack the maple logs in the shed. It would heat their house for two seasons. I separated the long, smooth branches from the rest and set them aside; I planned to spend next weekend sanding them down into perfect walking sticks. I helped Dad pick out the particularly beautiful pieces of maple, because he wanted to make cutting boards as Christmas gifts. Mom spent the afternoon raking up the sawdust, which she wanted to use in the barn for the horses, and my siblings and I tossed the ugly bits into the stack of wood we kept at the back of the property for campfires and gathered the moss and mushrooms that came with the maple's rotting bits and put them into the compost heap, a crucial resource for us in the springtime.

We must take from the natural world to survive, but how we do it makes all the difference. I found it difficult to mindfully participate in tree planting, which to me felt like just another profit-making endeavour. I was asked to plant mainly one-year-old pine seedlings in Prince George, Chetwynd and Tumbler Ridge, as pine is more profitable when the area gets logged again. I wasn't replanting a forest; I was replanting what John Vissers might call a monoculture and what I felt was a future site of destruction, where slash piles would grow higher and higher.

After a long day of tree planting, we would all make our way back to the truck to count our empty boxes and log our totals.

"How many did you plant today?" the foreman would ask us. The other planters proudly announced their numbers and talked about how they had conquered the terrain, scaling slash piles and adeptly manoeuvring around stumps, as turkey vultures circled above, squirrels chattered from beyond the tree line and horseflies and mosquitos buzzed around but too slowly to bite the planters barrelling over the barren landscape planting like wild beasts. *One, two, tree. One, two, tree. One, two, tree.* I would report my numbers to the foreman sullenly, becoming increasingly disillusioned with the practice I was participating in. We were paid cents per tree: fifteen or twenty cents if the terrain was markedly difficult—a steep incline, high slash piles or no slash piles but excessive tree waste scattered across the entire cutblock. The incentive was to plant as many as you could as fast as you could. No one got anywhere by pondering the state of where they were or what they might be unwittingly participating in.

Once we returned to camp, we socialized over dinner and beer and around a campfire. Slash piles, bone-white tree carcasses and torn land faded from their minds. I can't say I blame them. What would be the point of dwelling on an industry that doesn't want to change? But as we sat there, enjoying ourselves and taking in some much-needed rest after a long and difficult day, the atmosphere of being in a wooded area separate from the cutblocks began to overtake me. Eventually, the stars came out and the campfire cast a warm glow that illuminated the trees around us. Visions of Sumas Mountain, of hummingbirds and waterfalls, tall, wide trees and soft earth, delicate lady ferns and speckled mushrooms came rushing at me. Just as someone brought out a guitar and the entire crew began singing, I began feeling that my efforts to replant these shredded mountains might be in vain. The way these forests had been severed from their root systems for miles—the new crop could never be the same.

Maybe, though, that wasn't the point. Maybe we weren't there to help the earth replenish itself but rather to help a capitalist scheme grow certain trees in certain areas to a certain age so they can be harvested again. The crew sang, and I joined in from time to time, unable to tell them how I really felt. After a while, I stopped singing, no longer able to sit comfortably with my own youthful disillusionment.

I did not join the tree planters next summer. Instead, I spent that summer, and the one after that, and the one after that, and all the months in between, reconnecting with the forest. I decided I needed to listen to the trees, learn from them and work to observe how all the elements in the woods worked together. It was this dedication to connection that brought me, one autumn day years later, to a new trail up Sumas Mountain.

That day, I found myself wandering up a path lined with deciduous leaves yellowed with the onset of the season. I grew lost in thought. I listened to the chatter of the birds hidden in the thick sweetness of the decomposing autumn forest. With each step I breathed in cool air. I was in tune with each step, each breath or breeze, each turn of the trail, each chirp of a bird or a squirrel. After about an hour of walking, I came to the peak of a small hill. There, in the immediate distance, was a section of forest that had been completely levelled.

Observing a scene like this can physically hurt. My heart leapt as I left the fullness of the treed woods behind me and inched toward the fallen guardians scattered haphazardly and spray painted with a massive X. Some of the larger logs were labelled "Gary." Stumps were tinted red where the saws had bit into their flesh, cutting into them from both sides like open wounds, until they fell. One after another and another and another. Hundreds.

Sections of Sumas Mountain have been logged, in large and small chunks, since the late 1800s. I knew much of that logging provided for the livelihoods of families, yet I thought then, staring out at that quiet, decimated landscape, that there had to be a better way than clearcutting. Like high-grading, for example—the process of removing only the most valuable trees in a given area—although I knew most logging companies considered this too expensive of an endeavour. The cutblock, though, seemed to me then a perfect example of excess.

THE FLOOD

Know by the thread of music woven through
This fragile web of cadences I spin
That I have only caught these songs since you
Voiced them upon your haunting violin

—"Autumn's Orchestra," E. Pauline Johnson

November 2021, 11:00 a.m. Environment and Climate Change Canada issued a rainfall warning for Metro Vancouver and the Fraser Valley. Notices were posted for Whistler, parts of the Sunshine Coast and Howe Sound. This included Sumas Mountain. My home. *Haven't we had enough?* The hazard quoted in official reports was the expectation of between one hundred and one hundred and fifty millimetres of rainfall, compounded by the melting snow that came with unseasonably warm temperatures. All of this would increase natural river and creek flows, as well as mountain runoff. Localized flooding was anticipated. The scale of that flooding would be named a once-in-a-hundred-years catastrophe—a claim that I fear, as the rains fall heavier each time they come, as the dry, hot weather grows drier and longer each year, as climate catastrophes and climate weirdness become increasingly normal, will soon be outdated.

12:00 p.m. Rain slammed into the side of my house. It trashed the forest and pummelled the dry earth. I went outside to check the flow of water in the seasonal stream that runs through the backyard. From inside the dry safety of my living room, and over the roar of the rainfall on the tin roof, I could hear the tumbling water. In late fall and early winter months, this small creek typically flows gently past my front steps. The water can move along at quite a pace, but I had never seen a current like this. It was heavy and thick with mud and moved with steady force. Clad in green rain pants, boots and a matching fully buttoned knee-length raincoat, I raked out some of the leaves and debris to keep the flow unobstructed and avoid any unnecessary pooling. So far, the earth, surrounding forest and natural waterways that this stream passed by were doing their job; the water was under control—for now. But the heavier the rain fell, the more swollen my little stream became. The wider creek behind the property, deeper in the forest and which I crossed over daily, had reached enormously high levels.

We all witnessed this weather in awe. Neighbours wearing yellow, green and black rain jackets and Hunter rainboots met on the streets to compare details of how their backyards and springs and creeks and ponds were faring. Kids, swallowed by full-body Newt Suits and Muddy Buddy overalls, pulverized puddles as their parents spoke. Sheets of water fell from the sky, suffocating everything they touched. Someone said that the rainfall was being classified as an *atmospheric river*. Feeling the wind pick up, someone pointed to the tree tips bending like spaghetti noodles, twisting and turning and threatening to snap or pull. A Newt-Suit child fell over. Then another. Black clouds grew thick, and neighbours returned to their respective corners of the cul-de-sac to wait out the storm.

Throughout that day, biblical showers and wind hammered the house. I watched the trees hold onto the earth with their strong, steady roots, but their branches sailed past the windows as if I was in Dorothy's Kansas house. Then, just before 4:00 p.m., the weather lightened: the rain and wind slowed down enough to warrant a short meander outside to assess the damage.

I started with a jaunt around the property, first stopping at that typically manageable seasonal stream now met with three other sources of water. One came from the northeast side of the property, another from a natural spring directly north and the third came from a massive deluge of water, mud, sand and debris, diverted from what I'd later discover was a washout from the property directly above ours on the mountain. The small stream had become a heavy, rushing little river. Several feet wide and a foot deep, the river was moving fast enough to clear a toddler out of the way.

The section of land that was usually in my neighbour's property was now flowing steadily at my front steps. The neighbours had recently cleared some trees from this area and they had plans to take out more. I was struck by what happened to a small, levelled area in weather like this, a reality likely to continue and become worse in the future. I began to imagine what could happen to a larger cleared section of land.

Stepping in and around puddles and pools and pathways of water, I started toward the creek deeper within the forest. Along the way, flows ribboned over my boots; whatever land that had been touched by human, void of natural ground cover and root systems to keep the earth in place—walking paths, old logging roads, clearings where tractors came to harvest fallen trees—had turned to a soupy mess. Whatever section of land that had remained naturally treed and thick with underbrush was relatively the same as it was before the storm, with only a glossy wetness blanketing the forest. The closer I got to the creek in the woods, away from the flooding on the property, wading through drenched trails, the louder the water flow became. I could hear from several hundred feet away the crashing of waves and boulders slamming into one another as the current moved. Coming around the final corner, I saw the flow that matched that torrential noise.

This creek, which was diluted to a trickle that summer, had breached and carved out new banks. It barely held what was the widest and highest water level I had ever seen. The bridge—made from cement blocks, heavy beams and six-inch iron nails, notably high above the surface of the regular water level—had been washed out, long gone. The only evidence it had ever been there was a single twisted nail sticking out from a beam embedded in the still-intact soil at the river's edge. Young vine maples and cedar trees, who had not yet had the chance to develop strong root systems along the shore, came loose and were pushed down beneath the river's surface, scraped clean by tumbling boulders, the red under their bark a sharp contrast to the frothing brown water. The force of the water dislodged these boulders—the size of wheelbarrows and larger—and they resettled precariously elsewhere. The terrible rock-on-rock and rock-on-wood noise added an eerie, skull-crushing tone to the chaos of it all. Eddies swirled and carved new divots in the land, eroding roots and soil. The creek had been reborn.

Was this all rainfall? Was snowmelt to blame? I speculated as I stood in shock along the shore of this normally gentle waterway. *Perhaps*, I thought, *logging and damming farther up the mountain were also causes.* Like a domino effect, one change to the natural process of water management can have a great impact. There is always someone or something downstream.

The chaos continued: roads across Sumas Mountain and in other areas in Abbotsford were closed. Washouts caused erosion beneath the pavement where culverts could not manage the water running through them—the overflow ran over and around instead, cutting away at the road's underbelly. Warnings of further flooding and evacuation alerts went out. Farther down the mountain in the valley where Sumas Lake had once bloomed, the Trans-Canada Highway was closed in both directions: in a matter of a few short hours, the highway had flooded, cutting off Abbotsford from its neighbouring city, Chilliwack. People were stranded. A state of emergency was declared as schools closed and homes were evacuated. The livestock that farmers could not save in time were stranded.

By the next morning, it looked in part as if Sumas Lake had returned to Fraser Valley. Locals worked with the Canadian Armed Forces to ensure the Barrowtown pump station remained operational. If this went, the Fraser River would flow into the valley and many more animal lives and properties would be lost. The gas pipeline was shut off and local petrol rationing was put in place. A Tiger Dam was built along the sections of the highway not yet flooded. As members of our community—and eventually the Canadian military—worked hard to keep the water at bay and the pump functioning, the rest of us could do nothing but wait. Wait and watch. Wait and see what the fate of our town would be.

When it was all over, one estimate stated that close to 600,000 chickens, 400 dairy cattle, 12,000 pigs and 3,000,000 bees were drowned. *What about the wild animals?* I thought. *Where are their statistics? How many of them drowned in their homes?*

Over the next fifteen days, there were three atmospheric rivers in the valley and water levels continued to increase. Boats were deployed where roadways and farms once were, collecting stranded people from their second- or third-storey bedroom windows. My backyard river and the deluge of water and mud coming from logged portions above was nothing compared to the tumultuous flooding that will be felt in BC for years to come.

Upon waking early on the Saturday that followed the catastrophic flooding, I was surprised to see puffy white flakes of snow drifting down from the greyness above. The snowfall continued throughout the morning and into the early afternoon, a softening silence arriving with each fallen flake. This quiet was a welcome distraction from the climate weirdness barrelling through the Fraser Valley, yet I knew this would only add to the trauma of those whose farms and homes may still be under water.

That winter, after the final piece of a three-ringed circus was mounted—COVID-19; that summer's heat dome and frenzied forest fires; flooding on a near-biblical scale—we finished the year with snow and ice. Feeling the weight of that year one bitter afternoon, G. and I went for a walk.

We started along that familiar trail through the woods on Sumas Mountain that begins at the back of the property behind the woodshed. The path runs down an old logging road that is barely perceptible unless you know where to look. The road, if you can call it a road by today's standards, leads to a trailhead, which then leads through a tangle of deciduous and coniferous woods, over the creek on a wide bridge and then around a small waterfall. You can stay there and enjoy that cascading plume of mist or you can branch onto another route. There is a network of soft earthen paths meandering from here to the many corners of Sumas Mountain. One loops around the mountain, behind the neighbours' properties and into deeper forests before returning to Charlie Spruce Place. G. and I decided to follow that one.

G. and I followed the old logging road, uneven and pitted with mud craters. We took great care not to lose a boot. Treeless mountainsides, excessive rainfall and the overflowing of the creek left the soil along our path deeply carved and widened, with a residue of mud, sand and tree branches. The ground was littered by uprooted sword ferns, rocks big and small, and tiny bits of garbage—shiny granola bar wrappings, a deflated blue balloon, mud-encased plastic bags and a six-inch plastic green velociraptor. Looking closely at where we stepped, we could see the ghostly mark of fast-running water in places it shouldn't have been. These remnants told a story of a large current flooding the trail, finding the lowest points and uprooting whatever was in its new-found path.

Farther along, we could still hear the roar of the creek. It wasn't as loud as the day of the flood, yet the closer G. and I came to the water the more evidence of a much-changed space was revealed. Roots raw from being chafed, scraped and dinted by rocky, sandy water exposed the underbelly of bark ripped away and the red sores of torn flesh beneath. The land that normally covered those roots, protecting them from exposure, had been completely carved away, a process that left deep gashes in the roots, trees and land itself.

The creek was unrecognizable. Inspecting from the new water's edge, we saw the massive new boulders that came from somewhere above to replace what had been washed away. If a walker was nimble, she could hop from one boulder to the next, making her way across to the other side, but it was impossible to know how sturdy or slippery these rocky mammoths were. G. and I skipped the boulder hopping and instead made our way across downstream. There, too, the creek had changed: what was once a sandy pool no more than a foot deep, where we came to cool our feet during the warm summer months and where horses, dogs and kids could easily cross, was now a tumbling, rock-strewn, hissing, wide and deep section of the creek. It had gained ground at least three feet on either side, cutting into the root base of trees lining the bank; those trees were barely standing. The only way across was the newly strung-up cable-and-wood-slat suspension bridge, with a rope above it to hang onto if one's bravery needed support.

I went first and G. followed. The bridge swayed; a lousy balance or one false step could send the crosser into the water and the newly laid stone minefield below.

Once across, with very little drama as it turned out, we wandered up the path and away from the creek, in the same direction we had always gone. The route, though, continued to be nearly unrecognizable to our seasoned eyes. The waterfall looked like one I had never seen before, yet it was the same one I have visited time and time again since I was a young girl.

I imagined countless birds and squirrels and other critters whose lives and homes had been destroyed. I wondered who managed to get out in time. As we turned away from the waterfall and continued down the path, G. and I acknowledged how lucky we had been. Our home was still standing. None of our beloved animals or personal items had been dragged away. We were dry and safe. Unlike so many others. For a time, we talked as we walked. We talked until there was nothing left to say, and then we continued in silence.

Remnant Waters

When the rainfall stopped and the rivers once again remained in their riverbeds, I went for a hike up the south side of Sumas Mountain to catch a higher glimpse of the devastation. When I got to the top, to what we call Donnie's Point, I could see the valley below. The flood water had yet to recede. I saw the wreckage that spread from east to west—and the ghostly beauty of what Sumas Lake once was.

The heavy continuous rainfall that caused the Sumas Dike and Nooksack River to breach had ceased that morning. The sun rose in the eastern sky, stretching its way toward Vancouver in the west, as I ascended Sumas Mountain. Near the top, I stepped off the main trail and onto the shorter route to the edge of a cliff that overlooks the prairie. Instead of a highway, checkered farmlands and large barns and homes scattering the valley floor—a sight I always anticipate—the prairie was a large blanket of water. The surface sparkled as the sun came up in the east, casting long shadows of copper sunrise across the rediscovered lake as it rose higher and higher. The "lake" reached as far as Vedder Mountain and the North Cascades across from me. Taking out a pair of binoculars, huddled with a pair of gloves in my jacket pocket, I examined the damage below.

Scanning from left to right, I could spot just above the water's surface the metal roofs of dairy and poultry barns. In some cases, the top floors of residential houses were spared and I saw a single window above the water. A few fortunate farmhouses were on what now looked like tiny land islands—little rare mounds of earth in the flat valley now dry but stranded. Boats motored where fields once were, stopping in various places for a few moments before continuing somewhere else. I'd heard that in the early mornings and near dusk before evening set in, when the light is best at hiding those who are up to no good, some opportunists were looting family farms, stealing supplies, equipment, family heirlooms and diving for safes; I wondered whether the boaters I saw from my perch on the mountain were helping people or adding to the chaos and stealing.

The highway that connects Chilliwack to Vancouver was a snaking river between submerged trees, buildings and billboards. A red SUV, a black pickup truck, a long-haul semi and various other vehicles—marooned on higher parcels of land surrounded by water—sat abandoned along the missing road. Somewhere in the distance, black smoke plumed and drifted through the valley air. A parade of fire trucks drove on a stretch of dry road far in the distance and half a dozen helicopters—the most I had ever seen in one place—flew above it all. They were in the process of rescuing those stranded in their homes, carrying supplies to and from farms whose livestock was alive but left behind, assessing damage and reporting the events to the rest of the world.

If I turned my binocular gaze downward directly below me, I could examine the Sumas Dike. In several places, water flowed over the dike in a steady stream. To the east, trucks and machinery were working to build up the dam. A parade of dump trucks, one after another, drove on dry roads, isolated from the flooded areas, to reach the dike. They lined up on the sandy island and waited for their turn. One at a time, when given a signal, they drove forward to their designated spot, dumped their load, then backed up to the beginning before turning around and heading back for more. The work appeared endless to me as I scanned the valley, seeing flashing lights, emergency vehicles, abandoned cars with their lights still on, boats screaming from place to place and a pink flamingo inner tube, an absurd memory of an absurd summer, drifting alone amidst it all.

The view was one of misery, chaos, death and destruction—and as I caught a trumpeter swan in the binocular's gaze gracefully land into the water, carving a wide V in its wake, I saw something close to beauty. The natural world—the elements that had survived, anyway—were reclaiming this flooded water as the lake that once was, while all around it was mayhem. I could not ignore this contrast. Watching the scene play out before me, I began to feel an out-of-body experience. I could not grasp how this could have happened, knowing what we know about extreme weather: we'd all been privy to news about environmental disasters around the globe directly linked to human-driven climate change. Did we think we were absolved from feeling its impacts here in the developed world? Were we so untouchable?

I grew frustrated by our inaction to mitigate this flood and guilty at my own participation in overtaking land—and I was also awed by the stunning picture the "lake" provided. I couldn't rectify the different ways I felt looking down at the valley. We cannot reclaim the lake in the form it once was: the farmland beneath it is too precious and necessary now. But we cannot continue down the path we are on, making changes and taking from the environment without considering the impacts of those changes. If I put the binoculars away and ignored the helicopters circling above, I could see the valley below without the chaos—but I could still feel it brewing all around and emanating from inside me.

WINTER

It reaches to the Fence—

It wraps it Rail by Rail

Till it is lost in Fleeces—

It deals Celestial Vail

— "It Sifts from Leaden Sieves," Emily Dickinson (1862)

Rescue

As the days grew shorter, I struggled this year to see the beauty and cheer that winter can bring. We were heading into another season, another period rife with the potential for extreme weather, and I was tired. We were all tired. It was for this reason that I decided, with my family, that building wreaths was more important than ever.

In the winter months, it is tradition for my family to collect castoffs from rescued garden flowers and tree branches and pinecones. We gather the broken limbs of coniferous cedar and fir and pine, accumulating bunches from around the circumference of our property and along the trails behind our home. I prefer the ones with huddles of cones still attached—they make a nice gathering spot on the circling shape of wreaths, where bows can be tied and where we can start to weave dried flowers and red berries from the mountain ash tree and spiky, glistening green leaves from a holly tree.

In November, the wreath building begins. I like to hang those traditional circular-shaped wreaths on the front door. My mother builds wild swags with wide, drooping cedar branches and all manner of found foliage attached by a plaid bow. She takes them to her relatives' resting places in Vancouver's Mountain View Cemetery. This annual visit, making the swag and gently transporting it from Sumas Mountain to Mountain View, then participating in the Remembrance Day ceremony that occurs there each year, indicates for us the start of winter. It is a chance to connect and to demonstrate our gratitude for those who have fallen. With these swags, we bring a piece of Sumas Mountain to our ancestors, connecting our lives to theirs the best way we know how.

As the onset of winter draws nearer—sometimes during an early snowfall and sometimes during relentless rain—we make more swags and wreaths. With hot chocolate, mulled wine and hot apple cider brewing on the stove (we like to have our options), the scent of clove and cinnamon circulating every inch of the house, we stoke the wood stove before each of us brings our own materials to the kitchen table. We assemble them any way we like.

For my wreath, I use wire from an old closet hanger and bend it into a circular shape. Then, I select the first tree branch to use as the foundation upon which all other pieces will attach. Often, I choose the nimble cedar. Its long, lacy branches smell warmly sweet as I entwine them with the wire. Where it doesn't like to bend or stay, I use a small hemp string to attach it to the wire with a tiny bow. When the entire wire is no longer visible from the front, I add pieces of fir and pine—much smaller and clustered with cones, these are secured with red plaid or green silk bows and more hemp. Next comes the colouring: dried red berries from mountain ash, smooth, shiny and spiky bunches of green from the holly and now and then a dried dahlia or echinacea or Autumn Joy sedum flower. I never use glue to attach on the wreath as I return each of the natural elements back to the forest and keep the wire for next year. In the end, each year, I have an entirely different wreath to hang on my front door.

These wreaths help bring my family closer. I see them as a celebration of the abundance and circularity of life on Sumas Mountain. They signal the winter months and bring the outside world closer to us as we get cozy inside. The wreath reminds me that those cast-away pieces that fall to the ground and dry up in the transition from summer to fall and winter or are drowned by heavy waters can still be beautiful, repurposed and anew. *And you do not need much energy*, I think to myself as I tie on the last bow of this year's wreath, feeling heavy with the weight of the year myself, *to make one.*

I DREAM OF STORMS

In the winter of 2017, the Fraser Valley endured an ice storm. Heavy snow and ice blanketed the land. Massive trees bowed and shattered under tremendous weight. Shrubs and ferns were encased like museum pieces, powerlines snapped, ponds, wetlands and creeks froze, and a crystallized film, patterned with the delicate swirls left by air and water, dressed everything the cold snap touched. Even the creek behind our house had grown stiff: the surface was glassy and thick with the bulbous remnants of air and water bubbles. Small frozen waves curled up and under themselves. If I listened closely, I could hear the slight gurgling of flowing water beneath the surface, muted by the two feet of ice I stood on. I'd never seen anything like it in my life on Sumas Mountain. I was told this was a once-in-a-hundred-year phenomenon. Four years later, it happened again.

The winter holidays were nearly over. December celebrations closed behind us and New Year's Eve was approaching. Trees still twinkled in living room windows and white and coloured lights lined rooftops. Winter lawns donned blow-up Santa Clauses, their generators humming long into the night, pumping air into soft bodies, giving them life.

Families gathered for dinner, gift giving and merrymaking as the memory of the summer heat dome, the fall flooding and the pandemic had begun to fade ever so slightly, replaced by the sparkle and wonder of winter. For some, the warmth of the holidays provided a much needed if temporary amnesia of the events of 2021. The promise of a new year brought hope for a fresh start. This fresh start, though, arrived with yet another slam of winter weather, tossing the last hopes of *maybe next year will be different* out the window.

Weather warnings had been trickling in across the Fraser Valley over the last few days of December. Meteorologists promised that the onset of the next dire weather system would hit on the first of January. They said it would start with snow, coming in fast from the coast and moving inland, followed by freezing rain and strong winds. On December 31, as the afternoon rolled in, G. and I fed the living room fire with a large walnut log, checked the pipes for any freezing, brewed a batch of mulled wine, washed the dishes and settled in with slippers, housecoats and red-and-white reindeer pyjamas.

It began slowly. My family and I were safe and warm in our home, and the scent of cloves and cinnamon permeated the air as the glow of the barrel-shaped, cast-iron wood stove sent bright flashes up our living room walls. As the light outside dimmed, evening closed in. Night pressed up against the windows, and as I looked out at the black and grey woods, it seemed that the forest was leaning in too. Then silence came, as if the entire mountain knew what was coming.

The snow had begun earlier in the day, just as the last light sunk behind the horizon, leaving streaks of pastel pinks and greys along the fringes of the woods. It was unhurried in the beginning. Steady but with leisure, bits of lace floated down gently among the Douglas firs, almost like in a dream. We saw it rest on cedar boughs and naked maples and gather on the grass and fence rails. Slowly, snow blanketed everything in a layer of white fleece. But after a time, as the last pink rays vanished, leaving a murky grey, the precipitation increased. The snow became fat, heavy and wet. Then darkness came. By the time we'd settled in to await the outcome of the storm warning, the moon and the stars had hidden beyond the veil of winter sky; only a lonely porch light illuminated a single section of sky and thick falling snow. The little bits of lace that were so pretty and delicate in the beginning had turned into an indecipherable cloud of white. It became nearly impossible to tell where a flake began and another ended; it all fell as one, together and relentless.

Other regions in Canada and around the world are accustomed and often prepared for intense snowfall like this. I have read stories about prairie winds and snows in Manitoba and Saskatchewan, of men and women in early settler days tying ropes from their cabins to the outhouse across the yard. They would clutch the rope during extreme weather to get from one place to the other; if they let go, they'd be lost in the blizzard. I learned about young kids in Ontario and Montreal getting lost in winter months and of animals in a Texas sanctuary found frozen to death after storms settled. I'd heard about snow drifts that swallow entire vehicles, trapping people inside, and of snowfalls that bury houses. Some of these areas have learned to expect extreme weather like this.

Their snowplows stand at the ready as linemen crews prepare for power outages and local people anticipate the harshness that comes with winter in their hometowns. Snowfall is not unheard of on Sumas Mountain; there had certainly been white Christmases throughout my lifetime and the lifetimes before me. But our community was far from prepared. This was extreme weather for us, and as I looked up at the dark sky as the flakes swirled and the wind picked up, wrapped in a wool blanket and safe behind the windowpane, I grew increasingly concerned. I was grateful to be warm and safe, but these "strange" weather events were becoming not so strange. Their frequency, weirdness and unpredictability worried me. How are the less fortunate keeping warm? How do the sparrows and cardinals and deer prepare for and survive these extremes?

I dreamt that night of storms, of snowdrifts that suffocate and of becoming lost in a white wilderness. I dreamt I was a red squirrel, huddled cozy and warm in my burrow. Nuts were piled high, lining the walls. A thick layer of insulation surrounded me as I slept the night away. When day broke the next morning, I awoke and remembered my humanness. The storm had finished.

The early morning sky was still dim and grey. After a hot cup of coffee, G., our dog Charlie and I geared up in tall boots, gloves, winter jackets, hats and scarves and stepped outside to assess the new winter world that had arrived.

The morning was frigid: the mercury thermometer on my deck read -20°C. The average temperature at this time of year is zero. When G. and I stepped outside, snow drifts had blown up the front stairs to the landing and reached into the covered entryway, piling up along the edges. This was our first task: shovelling the drifts and clearing a path down to the ground.

With a pathway established, we checked the pipes at the side of the house. Not frozen yet. We poked around at the sections strapped with electric heat tape and those with insulating foam and flipped on the little heater nearby. These pipes had frozen before without causing too much trouble, but I knew there was danger of burst pipes. All was clear so far, so we decided to take a walk in the woods.

It was early and mostly overcast, yet glimmers of blue began peeking through the clouds here and there, offering promises of a brighter day. We picked up our maple walking sticks standing in the woodshed, protected from the brunt of the snow, and went into the woods. As we passed the tree line, trying our best to remember and follow the now-hidden path, trees heavy with fresh snow closed in around us. Sweeping cedar boughs bent over to touch the white ground, blocking the path in places and forcing us to step around or under. From time to time, we'd tap a low hanging branch, shedding powder and shooting the lightened branch back to its original place. With G. walking in front of me and Charlie trailing behind in our wake, I saw an opportunity to tap a branch above him as he ducked beneath, sending a shower of snow down the back of his neck.

The walk was slow as we trudged our way through several feet of fluffy snow. *Step, step, step* Charlie and I went, following the ploughed path of G. the leader in front. As we

came to the creek, we could hear the muted gurgling of rushing water—muted because of the heavy snow piled on top
of a thin layer of ice. We stepped closer and, reaching the
edge, were careful not to step on the surface of the creek
itself. Instead, we listened. The snow subtly muted the forest; we felt as if we were in a snow globe. We heard that
bubbling creek, then the twittering of a snowbird. Snow fell
from a tree branch in the woods somewhere nearby, producing a faint *thud*. Just as we were about to assess where to
cross to the other side, the skies moved. Through a crack
in the dull grey ceiling of cloud, a glimmer of sunlight shot
outward, landing on the surface of the snow-covered creek.
Instantly, a million glistening diamonds shuddered with the
ever-so-slightly-brightening light. We watched as that sky
continued to part, revealing blue clarity and that certain kind
of distant and cold sunlight that only appears in winter. It
was pure magic. Then, as if someone switched on a disco
ball, the entire forest, covered in layers upon layers of snow,
shimmered. It came alive with light and movement, inhaling and exhaling that glisten and glint of millions of unique
patterns of snowflakes, all combining to create a one-of-a-
kind quilt of snow. We remained there for a time, standing on
the threshold of the creek just beyond the path. We watched
and listened, feeling the expansive beauty that only comes
with a fresh snowfall. Then, as if the woods were telling us it
was time to move along, a branch snapped above us, sending
an embarrassed red squirrel squawking and jumping to another branch, and then another and another, until he found
his balance. He flew high above us, sending snow cascading

down around us, confirming our illusion that we had entered a snow globe. But we took the hint; off we went.

Carefully stepping on revealed stones not yet fully blanketed, we made our way across the creek and continued along the path through the pillowy forest. Our destination was a view; we called it Donnie's Point because it was discovered by our neighbour Don. Without the snow, it would typically take us about forty-five minutes to reach the top. Trudging through the white stuff, growing deeper as we climbed the mountain, we reached the summit in two hours. There, on a clear day, you look out to a sweeping view of the valley below Sumas Mountain. The view spans straight ahead, south to the US border, with Chilliwack to the east and the rest of the valley to the west, and mountains encasing it all. On that snowy morning, as we found our way to the edge of Donnie's Point, we looked out into the vast stillness. We were perched like miniature figurines on a miniature mountain overlooking the valley below; every inch, stretching from the coast, through the valley and into the eastern mountains, connected by white.

Not a word was spoken as we watched the world, completely still. Aside from the faint blinking of a distant snowplow and the occasional truck, there was little traffic that we could see on the snow-covered roads. Hardly any life stirred in the trees. We breathed in the icy silence and watched in awe as the sunlight transformed the valley and mountains from the shadowy blue and white into a rare amber jewel. The mountain across the valley from us began to glow with morning sun. We stood in silence for so long that we witnessed that brilliant radiance soften. Then, the sky grew dimmer, a slow onset of cloud cover hiding the sun. More snow was coming.

Watching the rays diminish, we reluctantly decided it might be time to turn back. As we took one last look at the valley below, a single snowflake floated down just in front of me; I followed it with my eyes as it fell to the earth. When I looked up, the air had turned white with flurries. It was time to go.

By the time we wound down the mountain, across the frozen creek, behind the woodshed at the edge of our property and back home, the snow was really falling. It was wet and sloppy. Whatever part of us wasn't covered by waterproof clothing was soaked. Only a warm bath and a hot cup of tea could help us now. I opened the door and was grateful to meet the indoor warmth. Our cheeks were red and eyelashes crystalized. We flung off our coats and boots with grumbles of misery and relief. Charlie went straight to her favourite spot next to the wood stove. My hat had soaked through: wet, cold hair was plastered to my head and any exposed ends had grown icicles. I hung it on a rack next to Charlie. Next were my socks. My boots—adequate during the winter weather we usually get on the mountain—were too low for the too-deep snow. My grey socks were saturated with melt. Layer by layer, I peeled off what was soaked through or damp, hanging it to dry next to my hat and Charlie.

I decided to run a warm bath to defrost myself. Once the tub was full enough, I dipped one toe into the steaming water, and then a full foot. That tingling sensation was close to painful. It felt hot and icy all at once. Slowly, slowly, slowly,

I submerged myself into the water. Raised goosebumps textured my skin, protesting at the sudden change of temperature, then eventually subsided. Joy and comfort set in as my body began to thaw.

That December, Abbotsford saw fifty-seven centimetres of snow. A standard December will get approximately eight centimetres. Over the next several days following that initial storm, Sumas Mountain experienced a mixture of snow, ice rain and sun. After the storm passed, the entire Fraser Valley was encased in ice. The combination of freezing and melting, snowing and raining, heavy winds and drastically changing temperatures produced a series of weather-related catastrophes. Power lines came crashing down under the weight of the ice; across the city, people were left without power for anywhere between three to five days, depending on their neighbourhood. Roads were slick, and cars were parked in all sorts of strange places as their drivers tried in vain to get where they needed to go but ultimately had to leave their cars wherever they stood. On sunny days, mounds of snow turned soft and brown on contact with mud, then stiffened up once again overnight, becoming hard as granite. Icicles hung from my roof, two or three feet long and several inches thick. A not-so-wonderful winter wonderland.

Eventually, the weather warmed enough to begin the slow melt. Snowmen built in those spare moments of sunshine grew skinny and emaciated, their carrot noses and stick arms drooping more each day. Snow melted and turned to puddles big and small and roads were broken up by the freeze, revealing large potholes and cracks in the asphalt throughout Abbotsford. By February, rain would arrive, the ice would be gone and so would most of the snow. Everyone would be eager to move forward with their lives, participating in the Lunar New Year, enjoying Valentine's Day, St. Patrick's Day, Easter and then spring break. We pushed ahead; we needed to.

QUIET

Early in the new year, the December storm still fresh in our minds and rain forecasted for coming weeks, we were indulged with one perfect snowfall. Much gentler than our recent winter experience, with this snow came a great and majestic silence that fell over the fields, trees and burrowing hideaways of wintering critters. The gravel mines weren't running and the quads weren't screaming through the woods. Snow had been falling gently for hours, adding to the unusual amount of snow already on the ground. As the day wore on and turned to dusk then night, with the fading light and the rising moon, this new snowfall, merciful and light, was a graceful white blanket covering the earth, leaving in its wake distilled soundlessness.

Wanting to bear witness to this quiet beauty, I stood in the white grass behind my house looking out into the trees. Suddenly, the dim glow of lights in houses, seen only in the periphery of my vision, went out. The entire mountain lost power. Relief washed over me as the constant pressure of electricity, its dull thrum constantly permeating the air, lifted. It's amazing how the nearly unnoticeable buzz of energy is distinguishable in its absence. The silence from the snow, from the dawning night and from the power outage was profound. I stood, hushed, watching snowflakes, among the millions, flutter around me. The purity of a winter quietude does wonders to unburden human minds and hearts.

After a breathless eternity, where the clock neither moved forward nor backward and time seemed to remain suspended in the snowfall, I turned to walk back to the house. I would stoke the wood-burning stove to keep me cozy on a likely powerless night. I had plenty of maple logs if I needed them. The warm glow would lull me to easily sleep.

As I walked, a shadow emerged in the distance. A neighbour had stepped outside for a moonlight walk down the silent street. A raised hand of acknowledgement came my way as they recognized my shape set against the moonlit snow, in the same way I recognized theirs. Then, like the fluttering of snowflakes in a light wind, other neighbours emerged from their temperate homes. They came down their driveways or across lawns, weaving past dormant fruit trees and frost-covered flower beds, emerging onto the street.

Snow-booted or snow-shoed, we met under the glow of the moon and remained silent for a time. Together, we breathed in the quiet coolness of the night until, in speechless agreement, we walked to the end of the road, taking in the white-covered trees and trackless blankets of snow. In the company of those who also appreciate these moments, my mind was allowed to drift. The crunch beneath our boots and the shuffling of snowshoes were the only sounds we heard that night.

It is of course inevitable that the snow's white will turn brown and dull, and the lustrous sheen of a crisp winter will become saturated with notorious West Coast rain. The gravel mine will run, grinding, crunching, beeping and blasting, spewing grey dust into the atmosphere. On those days, the magic of winter fades and what settles in its wake is the reality of the mountain as a resource. The sound from the mines and roads and houses seeps into the bare winter forest, reverberating off stark trees. Without the lush-green summer foliage to muffle the sound of progress, I am reminded on my walks through the woods that change is here, always here. It arrives ruthlessly and continuously, endangering the spirit of this place and robbing us of the remnant of what was. But in those moments, those last moments of quiet snowfall, everything else troubling our minds and our world was silenced too.

Seeing Differently

When I walk along the trails behind my home, winter trees are bare and the sounds of the woods, usually teeming with animal life, are limited to the high-pitched *seet, seet* of the chickadee, a permanent resident of the Fraser Valley, or the shuffle of the lone deer looking for a scrap of food in the barren woods. As I drift asleep some evenings, I will hear the yips and howls of resident coyotes; some days I'll see footprints of the elusive bobcat or cougar. Largely, though, the trails of winter are bare and quiet, free from much action, and offer the opportunity to walk and think. Most often, I think about how quickly this place has changed in my own lifetime.

Mine is a complex relationship with Sumas Mountain. I try to be an advocate for the space I knew as a child, yet I am part of the colonial story of this country. My ancestors came from Italy, Austria, Scotland, England and Switzerland and settled on the unceded land of Turtle Island, and this is how I came to be on Sumas Mountain. I am aware that I am likely nostalgic for a version of the mountain that was, from some perspectives, already indelibly changed for the worse. Abbotsford, the city in which Sumas Mountain stands, is expected to absorb 70 percent of the Fraser Valley's growing population over the next thirty years. I remember when my friends' parents would refuse to drive out to my family's homestead on account of the remoteness; the rate at which the area is developing is striking.

We are, of course, all contributing to the shrinkage of biodiverse areas in some way. I use logs from the forest to keep me warm in the winter and electricity from Abbotsford's grid to light my rooms. I have dogs and cats and horses who keep me company, not exactly indigenous creatures to this place. My car, electric but made from oil, follows paved roads that take me to and from the school where I work—across from the rec centre where I play, next to stop lights that keep me safe, run by power coming from stations occupying natural spaces. I take my car to visit friends out of town and to grocery stores filled with a mixture of local produce and packaged goods imported from all over the world. I purchase clothes to keep me warm, shoes to keep me dry and books to feed my mind, all housed in the growing number of shops scattered across Abbotsford. These consumer goods, too, are a mixture of local and internationally imported items. All these amenities that make my life easier and more comfortable infringe on natural spaces and biodiverse areas as their demand grows with increases in our population. This is our burden as humans. As I approach the creek on my walk, I sometimes crouch down at the edge of it and close my eyes. I desperately want to know how I, a settler, should approach and live on the land. I want to feel the earth as I struggle with this question, as I struggle to place myself in this world.

My presence on Sumas Mountain and that of my family—we have intruded into something far older than us. We are part of a story of commandeering space, privatizing and altering it to suit our own needs. I know this is part of my narrative. I wish it weren't.

I suppose all relationships are complicated once we closely examine them and the narratives that structure them. Perhaps we create these narratives to help us manage what we don't understand or what feels uncomfortable. Perhaps we sometimes create them to ease a sense of guilt, to ease the intuitive knowing of the destruction that humanity is capable of, a reality that some would like to shelve and ignore. So, we develop culturally sustained and socially enforced dialogues that allow for the continuance of what has been, to keep us moving in the same direction, because it's easier than the hard and difficult look at ourselves and the structures we live within; because it's easier than the critique of our modes of comfort.

What I do know is that the creek at my feet and the dirt beneath me, the rocks and the trees, the underbrush sitting below a thin layer of winter snow, has been here before any of us set foot upon it. At the same time, it is, has always been, continually changing, generating and regenerating itself. Dirt piles up, rocks move, rivers flow, trees die and grow. A human sees it at some point during this process and attaches a story to it. We are storytellers; it's what we do. With each change in the natural world, our narratives shift to accommodate that change. With each new generation, the way a place is known and remembered alters. I romanticize and miss that old yellow schoolhouse that once stood on Sumas Mountain Road. What did those who came before me miss? How did they remember this mountain I love?

As I dip my fingertips into the creek, I create a narrative for it and the mountain. In it are tales of natural disasters across centuries, tales of heat waves, plagues, catastrophic lightning bolts igniting fires that raged from one side of the mountain to the other. There are great floods that separated communities—communities of people and communities of trees and wildlife. I create a narrative about revival, too, and of forests with highly intelligent root systems that form networks between trees that communicate the whereabouts of animals and water sources, the strength of the wind, the presence of bacteria in the soil.

How can a person learn to listen to a mountain, to really *see* it and respect it—and not engage with it as a site of possibility, respected only because of what it could be used *for*? *I am trying my best to listen,* I want to tell the mountain. *I am trying to tell the most accurate story I can.*

Each time I walk in the forest, I challenge myself to see the space in a new way. First, I start by focussing not on the sights but on the scents instead. I take a moment and close my eyes. Cold, fresh ice in the winter, that crisp sensation you feel in your nose when you open a freezer door, and decaying maple leaves in the fall. Fragrant vines and flowers in the spring and the summer's sweet, dried pine needles on the hot, packed dirt. As I move through it, I am reaching for the air and it reaches back and touches me. With my eyes closed, I block out the visual of what I think I should see in a forest and instead start to visualize it using the information it brings to my other senses. By doing this in isolation, I can focus on illuminating other ways of seeing. I try to distance myself from expectation and what I have been conditioned to believe I should experience when I go to the woods. What exists beyond what the narratives I grew up with have told me to notice? I breathe deeply and exhale these opportunities. At the creek behind my house, when the sunshine grazes the earth, warming it ever so slightly, I smell the muddy froth of the cold water and the dirt beneath the snow—musty earth layered with fungus, decomposed maple leaves and forgotten, stashed-away walnuts. Sometimes, I smell that lack of scent that only comes with winter.

With my eyes closed and enveloped by stillness, what am I thinking? Are these thoughts my own experiences of nature or are they narratives cultivated by socially and culturally reinforced ideologies and perspectives?

Do I have the space within me to listen to the natural world?

How can I translate its beyond-human methods of communication?

Do the words "progress" and "profit" exist within this language? How does my own language render me complacent to the weight behind those words?

How does my busy modern life distract me from alternative ways of being and ways of doing, ways that could include the health of the forest, the water, the mountain and wildlife?

I open my eyes again. I stare into the murmuring water.

Its variety of tones—the bubbles, splashes, trickles and dribbles—rush over rocks then slow into calmer pools before flowing over the next rock and the next and the next, all the way down and beyond where I can see. I look for my face in the calm places of the creek. My reflection is there in one moment, staring back at me, before being erased by tumbling water in the next.

Often on my walks, I fall into a daze as the sights and sounds around me blend. Sometimes, the only way I am pulled out of it is by the ruckus of wildlife. Ravens, perhaps because of my stillness and unaware of my presence, will cackle to one another. There is a pair I've seen for some years now in this area. They are quite large and one has a few missing and jagged tail feathers that I can easily recognize. The most common sound they make is a gurgling croak that starts low at the back of the throat, then rises in pitch as their conversations seem to grow more intense. There is also a slow-toned *craw, craw*—a lazy squawk—and a quick-paced *woba-woba-woba* and *clack-clack-clack*. Ravens have been known to imitate the sounds around them, including human languages. As they chatter above me, I wonder if they speak the gurgle of the creek or the whistle of the wind.

What can these birds, this creek, this soil, this place, teach me? How can I do better? There is so much to learn and rekindle in our minds and hearts. Perhaps it starts with seeing. Perhaps it starts with listening. Perhaps it starts with a deep love of a single place.

Renaissance

In the New Year, with great hopes ahead of me, I also like to think about the past. What's in a year? I recall the worry of extended frozen days and nights and the confusion I felt when the valley flooded. I know I am becoming more and more disillusioned. I know I am trying to find a way out. I remember the suffocation and helplessness during the heat dome and the destruction of the wildfires. I remember the grief. I know this will shape how I move through the world in the years to come.

I also remember beauty—when ruin and regeneration strangely collide.

In late spring 2018, I took a drive to visit a friend in Ashcroft, BC. Heading east out of Abbotsford, I took the Trans-Canada Highway through Chilliwack and Agassiz. I continued along this road at the junction in Hope, then passed by Yale, Boston Bar, Lytton—only a few years before it would be levelled in the wildfire of 2021. Suddenly, like driving into another world, the hills and roadsides running along the Thompson River turned from green to a scorched pattern of grey, black and brown—a clue that I was getting closer to Ashcroft and Cache Creek, areas decimated by the 2017 Elephant Hill wildfire, which ran through 192,700 hectares of land in seventy-five days.

Much of the earth within the Elephant Hill area was unable to replenish itself as the seeds for new trees embedded below the surface were scorched and unable to germinate. The fire had burned too hot for too long.

Glancing at the Thompson River to my left and rocky hillsides marked by the skeletons of scorched trees to my right, I noticed a sprinkling of something purple amidst the ash heaps. I pulled over onto the shoulder to investigate. When I got out of the car, I saw purple fireweed scattering the landscape. I marched away from the road, casting up a plume of dust and ash up to my calves, and found myself amidst a field of tall, thin flower stalks. The bases of mature plants had narrow stacked green leaves; they looked like miniature willow trees. Their stems were tinged red and surrounded all the way up to a pointed top by little flowers, each with five purple petals, about the size of a nickel. The centre of each flower had long white styles and four magenta lobes at the end that stuck out and curled backward. A direct contrast to the dull earth they had popped out of, these flowers were bewitching. They were everywhere. The sun beat down on me hard in this shadeless terrain, but I stood there for a long time. The hillside was the meeting of destruction and beauty—perhaps, at least, the beauty of hope.

Epilogue

"What is the use of a house if you haven't got a
tolerable planet to put it on?"

— Henry David Thoreau's letter to Harrison Blake,

May 20, 1860

"What you find depends on what you look for," my father
once told me. So, what do I go looking for—*sensing for*—
when I take the well-worn path behind my house?

Ascending a slight hill, my feet stepping heel-toe on the
dirt path, I smell the accretion of the seasons. Spring, summer,
fall, winter—the seasons are all here at once. I am walking
amongst them, stepping through dormancy and aliveness, rot
and rebirth, pasts and futures. The trees in spring are at once
bare and blooming, their sweetness permeating the air. The
ground is strewn with the decaying remnants of fall leaves
trapped beneath winter snow—and the next moment, that
debris is giving way to new life once more.

I close my eyes and hope to hear the whispers of this
place. Silence. Then, as my ears adjust, the chitter chatter
of birds and the *peep, peep, peep* of a chipmunk. The slither
of a yellow-striped garter snake in the underbrush. A breeze

teases the ends of my hair. The rain falls onto the canopy. The snow muffles everything into a stillness. A thunderous *boom* in the distance. The crunch and grind of the juggernaut of progress. The chipmunk's *peep, peep, peep* morphs suddenly into the *beep, beep, beep* of a reversing truck in the distance. To the right, the *pop, pop, pop* of a nail gun. A coyote howls to the moon, accompanying the squeal of an accelerating motor up Sumas Mountain Road. A lawn mower's cry cracks a frozen, muddy puddle at my feet.

I am sensing for and toward the remnants of the past we are sometimes too desperate to leave behind and in which I believe lie answers. I hope we will always keep a remnant, have something we feel worth saving. Standing in the shadow of a bigleaf maple tree—with bright-green buds that become deeper green and then white-spotted with mildew, shrivel and detach from its branch, now covered in snow, right before my eyes—I am aware I am standing before the remnant of greatness in this place, the keeper of a sense of time I cannot understand.

ACKNOWLEDGEMENTS

"Your notion of diverting your daughter's lively mind
and of teaching her to observe such agreeable and
varied objects as plants seems to me excellent."
— The first letter from Jean-Jacques Rousseau to
Madeleine-Catherine Delessert, August 22, 1771

The initial conception for this project came from a desire to understand the spirit of a place, to hold in writing its identity the best I know how and in hopes of communicating the deep interconnection that exists in a place like Sumas Mountain. What it turned into was a wider conversation around sustainability, climate change, growth and progress, naming and ownership, a history of family and the hope for a legacy that will outlive whatever changes the future brings, all through an intimate observation of those entities living within and contributing to a complex and important eco-system.

This project came to fruition not because I put pen to paper but because of the many voices, lives, histories and realities that set a foundation upon which the ideas presented here could be realized, cultivated, nourished, worked through and completed to the best of my ability. As such, there are many branches of gratitude that must be acknowledged.

First, I must respectfully acknowledge that I wrote this project on the unceded Traditional Territories of the Semá:th People of the Sumas First Nation, the Matsqui First Nation and the Stó:lō Nation. Stó:lō peoples have lived in this area for over ten thousand years as the original caretakers and custodians of this Land. I am grateful for their knowledge and wisdom, through which I have come to learn so much.

I must also thank John Vissers for his steadfast fight to protect this place and patient voice in telling the history of this area. Gratitude goes also to my parents, Rick and Sandy Lang, for their cultivation of community, patient ears and willingness to share stories. Thank you also for teaching me how to respect, care for and love the natural world. And to those residents of Sumas Mountain who honour the land upon which they live and who work to understand the deep interconnectedness of the forest upon which all life depends—thank you.

Thank you to those in the Graduate Liberal Studies program at Simon Fraser University; to Sasha Colby, Stephen Duguid and my fellow students, whose long-suffering patience helped me work through many chapters and sections included in this book; and to Richard Mackie at the *British Columbia Review* for your encouragement in pursuing this memoir.

Enormous thanks go to Vici Johnstone, Holly Vestad and the rest of the team at Caitlin Press. Your keen eye, most welcome encouragement, direct criticisms and belief in this project were invaluable.

Gratitude must also be extended to you who listened as I went over and over and over how to phrase the ideas embedded in these many paragraphs and pages. As I carried this book along with me in my mind, in every conversation, everywhere I went, you walked alongside me and were kind, patient, thoughtful and infinitely helpful.

And finally, thank you to Sumas Mountain. For the hours and days and months and years I spent wandering through your forests, along the edges of creeks, seated among moss and flowers and leaves and stones and trees, in wind and rain, winter and spring, through flood and fire, heat and ice, through the devastation of land loss and the ever-changing nature of this place, thank you for showing me how the forest breathes.

Forever grateful, Natalie Virginia Lang.

ABOUT THE AUTHOR

Natalie Virginia Lang is a Canadian writer and teacher, living on Sumas Mountain in Abbotsford. She is ardently dedicated to the preservation of natural spaces and continues to reflect upon the beauty and mystery of nature. Natalie has written several book reviews for *The BC Review* and has won multiple awards from Simon Fraser University for her work in the Graduate Liberal Studies department, and from which she hold a Master of Arts degree. *Remnants* is her first book.